Cr

Howlers of all kinds – whether they be simple spelling mistakes, such as 'Our cat has fleas so it keeps on etching', or complete muddled-up nonsense, like 'Doggerel is a little puppy with a short tail and several pauses' make up this book. There's something for everyone, even a Crazy Misstakes quiz, and it's all guaranteed to keep you in stitches!

CRAZY MISSTAKES

Janet Rogers

Illustrated by David Mostyn

Beaver Books

A Beaver Original
Published by Arrow Books Limited
17-21 Conway Street, London W1P 6JD
A division of the Hutchinson Publishing Group
London Melbourne Sydney Auckland Johannesburg
and agencies throughout the world

First published in 1983
Reprinted 1984
© Copyright text Victorama Limited 1983
© Copyright illustrations The Hutchinson Publishing Group
1983

This book is sold subject to the condition that it
shall not, by way of trade or otherwise, be lent,
resold, hired out, or otherwise circulated without
the publisher's prior consent in any form of
binding or cover other than that in which it is
published and without a similar condition
including this condition being imposed on the
subsequent purchaser.

Printed and bound in Great Britain by
Anchor Brendon Ltd, Tiptree, Essex

ISBN 0 09 936660 6

Contents

1 'Police found safe under bed'

Mistakes often make headline news when, either through an unfortunate misprint, or a careless editor, newspapers end up making claims they didn't quite intend!

Parrot disease fears
RSPCA WILL ARRANGE PAINLESS END FOR OWNERS OF BIRDS

MAN FOUND DEAD IN GRAVEYARD

AUDIENCE TRIED TO RUIN PLAY BUT ACTORS SUCCEEDED

TROOPS WATCH ORANGE MARCH

ENRAGED BULL INJURES FARMER WITH AN AXE

LARGE HOLE DISCOVERED IN MOTORWAY –
EXPERTS ARE LOOKING INTO IT

MOTORISTS TO FACE HEAVIER PUNISHMENTS
Could be suspended from the wheel for three years

GIRL FOUND WITH A DETECTIVE IN HER BOOT

WOMAN KICKED BY HER HUSBAND SAID TO BE GREATLY IMPROVED

PASSENGERS HIT BY CANCELLED TRAINS

HOTEL BURNS DOWN – 200 GUESTS ESCAPE HALF GLAD

MORE MEN FOUND WEDDED THAN WOMEN

LEARN TO DRIVE AS YOU WATCH TV

LABOUR MP COLLAPSES IN COMMONS
Sitting suspended as he is carried out on stretcher

WOMAN FOUND DEAD IN SUITCASE
Foul play not suspected say police

20-YEAR FRIENDSHIP ENDS AT THE ALTAR

MAGISTRATES ACT TO KEEP THEATRES OPEN

DEAD POLICEMAN IN THE FORCE FOR 22 YEARS

ANNUAL FAT CATTLE SHOW – 300 ALDERMEN
MARCH TO CHURCH

BRIDE OF TWO MOUTHS SUES HUSBAND

MONTY FLIES BACK TO FRONT

EVANS SAYS CAPITAL PUNISHMENT ELIMINATES
HOPE OF REHABILITATION

EX-BEAUTY QUEEN ADMITS SHE IS A WOMAN

CHANNEL SWIM ATTEMPT: BOSTON GIRL'S
ARRIVAL IN LIVERPOOL

NEW YORK CITY ADOPTS NEW SLOGAN:
IT'S ZGREATEC XAFOY FOR ZGREATED NEW YORK

DOG IN BED SEEKS DIVORCE

PEER'S SEAT BURNS ALL NIGHT

PUPILS MARCH OVER NEW TEACHERS

MIDGET SACKED FROM BASEBALL TEAM CLAIMS
UNFAIR DISMISSAL

RICHARD BURTON TO TEACH ENGLISH AT
OFORXD

LUCKY MAN SEES FRIEND DIE

BOLTING HORSE SAVED AFTER FALL FROM PONY

BIG PENTWORTH WIN FOR QUEEN
Major success for Windsor cow

SENATE PASSES DEATH PENALTY
Measure provides for electrocution for all persons over 18

DEBATE ON HANGING SUSPENDED

VOLUNTARY WORKERS STRIKE FOR HIGHER PAY

GRAPEFRUIT LATE TELLING POLICE OF INJURED
MAN

THREE BATTERED IN FISH SHOP: MAN GAOLED
FOR ASSAULT

PEACE OR WAR DEEMED NEAR

ILL-TREATED BY WIFE
Husband cooked for thirty years

MAN CRITICAL AFTER BUS BACKS INTO HIM

COUNCIL CLAIM STREET WAS DEMOLISHED BY
ACCIDENT

MEDINA TO HAVE PARENT–TEACHER
ASSASSINATION

POLICE ANXIOUS TO INTERVIEW MAN WEARING
DARK CLOTHING AND NO RAINCOAT

SOUTHPORT A TOWN OF OLD PEOPLE
One in 6 over 65 grave problem

ONION PROSPECTS REPORTED STRONG

WOMAN DENIES COMMITTING SUICIDE

BACHELORS PREFER BEAUTY TO BRAINS IN THEIR
WIVES

POLICE MOVE IN BOOK CASE

LOCAL MAN HAS LONGEST HORNS IN TEXAS

FALSE CHARGE OF STOLEN HENS – POLICE ON A
WILD-GOOSE CHASE

POLICE DISBELIEVE A NAVAL STOKER WHO SAYS
HE IS NOT DEAD

PUTTING A BRIDE ACROSS THE RIVER TO COST
ONE MILLION POUNDS

RUNAWAY COW LANDS ON GREENHOUSE ROOF

BUFFALO SWEPT OFF FEET BY MENDELSSOHN
CHOIR

UNDERTAKER'S FAILURE – LET DOWN BY
CUSTOMERS

GREENLAND VOLCANO IN ERUPTION
By permission of *The Times*

COUNCIL 'DIGGING OWN GRAVE'
Smaller body urged

PRISONERS ESCAPE AFTER EXECUTION

WOMEN ARE BECOMING MORE BEAUTIFUL MEN,
ALSO LOOKING BETTER SAYS SURVEY

WOMAN IS FATALLY MURDERED

FORMER GRAVEDIGGER BECOMES EDITOR OF
UNDERGROUND NEWSPAPER

IT'S ALL CISTERNS GO FOR THE NEW PROJECT

NUDE MAN WITH SHOTGUN CHARGED WITH
BEING IN POSSESSION OF A CONCEALED WEAPON

HAIR RESTORER STOLEN FROM LORRY ON M6
Police are combing the area

DOG BAN: MATRON TURNS DOWN POST

'COUNCIL PULLING BREAD AND BUTTER FROM UNDER OUR FEET' say local farmers and shopkeepers

200 NEW PRICE RISES, BUT GROCERS SAY THEY WILL NOT HIT HOUSEWIVES

TAX MAN CRUSHED IN ORANGE JUICE CASE

JULY BABIES FLOOD LOCAL HOSPITAL

COUNCILLORS TO TALK ABOUT RUBBISH

MANY ANTIQUES AT SENIOR CITIZENS' SALE

PRINCESS OF WHALES VISITS DOLPHINARIUM

FIDELIO ONLY OPERA BEETHOVEN WROTE ON MONDAY EVENING

CRITICAL CHEF HIT WIFE WITH WET MACKEREL

MAN FOUND GUILTY OF STEALING FOR THE GAS BOARD

GHANA TO CHANGE OVER TO DRIVING ON THE RIGHT
Change will be gradual, say government

Public Health problem
SPECIAL COMMITTEE TO SIT ON BED BUGS

COW SAVES A LIFE
Hauls farmer by tail from blazing building

FILM STAR FOUND DAD IN BATH

THE POPE SAYS HE HAS WAITED CENTURIES FOR THIS DAY

THIEVES STEAL 600 LOAVES FROM AN EMPTY DELIVERY VAN

THE ANNUAL SEARCH IS ON FOR THE BEST KEPT VILLAGERS IN GREAT BRITAIN

MAYORESS RECEIVES SOLID SILVER BRUSH AND BOMB SET

2 'A large lunch of tulips . . .'

Pick up any newspaper and you are certain to find something that has been misquoted, misprinted or misunderstood. Especially if it is a local newspaper and there is a mention of you, you can be certain that something will be wrong even if only your name! Mistakes can, however, make newspapers much more fun and here are some of my favourites. By the way, the names of the papers quoted here are those they had when they published the examples given. Since then some papers may have changed their names, or even gone out of business. Perhaps they made too many mistakes. . . .

'Before Miss Colverson concluded her concert with a rendition of *At the end of a perfect day* she was prevented with a large bouquet of carnations by the mayoress.'

Staffordshire Evening Standard

'A carpet was last night stolen from Ryde Council building. Measuring almost 6 square feet, the thief has baffled council officials.'

Sydney newspaper

15

'Unfortunately the Prime Minister left before the debate began, otherwise she would have heard some nasty comments about her absence.'

Lancashire evening paper

'Mr Smythe answers every anonymous letter he is sent, and makes sure the sender receives a reply.'

Oxford Mail

'*Today's weather:* A depression will mope across Southern England.'

The Guardian

'Recently Mrs Richards invested in a cow, and she is now supplying the whole neighbourhood with milk, butter and eggs.'

West Sussex Times

'Having spent over 46 years as production manager, and more than 50 years with the firm, Mr Albert Smail was present with a gold clock by Mr Arthur Brown, the boring shop attendant.'

Liverpool Courier

'Cynthia Bertross, the celebrated soprano, was involved in a serious road accident last month. We are happy to report that she was able to appear this evening in four pieces.'

Worthing Gazette

'Two bicycles that belonged to girls leaning up against a lamp-post were badly damaged.'

Glasgow evening paper

'The headmaster refused to comment on the situation but admitted that "some children here have been behaving very childishly".'

Baltimore Sun

'Colonel Marooney, the bottle-scarred veteran, died at his home last week aged 92.'

'Mr Clive Henderson of Dimchurch Avenue, played solo trumpet and was later awarded the medal for the best trombone player in the section.'

Sheffield Telegraph

'Nineteen-year-old Rodney Bennett set the world record by swallowing 192 live goldfish in 37 minutes in a San Antonio competition. His prize was a free fish supper.'

Toronto Sun

'He said that the printer had "read off the wrong line", but promised that arrangements were already in hadn ot heav tch netx editoin pirnted korrectly.'

Saturday Telegraph

'The bride's going away outfit was a powder blue crimplene suit with a matching coat, and brown accessories. Both are well known locally and belong to the church.'

Ely Standard

'In the upper sixth we have been trying to do away with school uniform altogether. I hope that soon we'll have the boys just wearing a tie and the girls a black skirt.'

Yorkshire Evening Post

'Mrs Manning was married before anaesthetics came into use in surgical operations.'

Cumberland Evening News

17

'Never throw away old chicken bones, or those left from a roast. Put them in water and boil them for several hours with a few diced vegetables, it will make very delicious soap.'

New Zealand Woman's Weekly

'Unless teachers receive a higher salary they may decide to leave their pests.'

The Times Educational Supplement

'Letters were sent to the 800 men. Each envelope was marked IMPORTANT in very large letters, so that those men who could not read might ask to have the letters read to them.'

American Digest

'The Ladies of the Merry Oldsters enjoyed a swap social on Friday evening. Everybody brought along something they no longer needed. Many ladies brought their husbands with them.'

Pennsylvania Post

'The statue of Sir Richard will now be looking down the transept of the aisle through bullet-proof glass for the first time in over 600 years.'

Daily Express

'Over 50 children took advantage of the mobile clinic and were examined for tuberculosis and other diseases which the clinic offered free of charge.'

Liverpool Echo

'Those who have never heard the Queen speak are always captivated by the beauty of her voice.'

Torbay News

'Grease stains on furniture may be removed with alkali, but old stains, being difficult to remove, must be tackled as soon as they are made.'

Woman and Home

'Parents and teachers are definitely to blame here. You find them playing on both main and by-pass roads, throwing each other's caps and dashing out after them, and many similar games.'

Lancashire Evening Post

'The villain made his escape from prison yesterday by helicopter. Police say they have set up road blocks and cannot understand how he has evaded them for so long.'

Daily Mail

'The way to his heart might lie in the tricky art of cooking his liver.'

She, cookery supplement

'Owing to a printer's error in last week's recipe for fairy cakes two ounces of "castor oil" was given instead of two ounces of "caster sugar" and we apologise for this mistake.'

Reveille

'Many diabetic children have learned to give themselves injections by the time they are tight.'

The Lancet

'For cockroaches do not use sodium fluoride, as children or cherished pets may eat the sodium fluoride instead of the cockroaches.'

Ludlow Tribune

'After consuming about a hundred portions of chips, 28 pounds of sausages, rolls, ice cream and cake, the Mayoress presented the trophies to the boys.'

Witham Times

'The referee called two policemen on to the pitch, and whilst the three were in discussion another hurtled over their heads.'

Exeter Express and Echo

'The new blouses are striped like a zebra, in black, scarlet, blue, green, yellow and mauve.'

Daily Sketch

'The Red Cross found a bed for him in an institution specialising in the treatment of artcritics.'

Colorado paper

'The font so generously donated by the Archer family will be placed at the North end of the Church. Babies may now be baptised at both ends.'

Berkshire paper

'Two men were admitted to hospital suffering from mild buns.'

Essex Weekly News

'In a bitterly cold wind, the Queen, wearing a warm sage-green tweed coat with a beaver lamb collar and a green mitre-installation of turbo-alternators and boilers.'

Thames Water News

'Last year 578,953 people visited the zoo, which was three times more than the previous year when no attendance figures were kept.'

American magazine

'Princess Margaret's daring but very fashionable hat caused quite a sensation when she opened a school for the blind at Sevenoaks.'

Tonbridge newspaper

'Mrs Norris, who won a brace of pheasants, kindly gave her prize bark and this raised £5.50 for the funds.'
Cambridge Evening News

'For some time past running water has been installed at the cemetery to the satisfaction of the residents.'
Reynolds' News

'If you ask six friends to name the commonest bird in Britain, nine out of ten will say the sparrow.'
Weekend

'The bride was gowned in white silk and lace. The colour scheme of the bridesmaid's gowns and flowers was punk.'
East Kent Times

'Unemployment dropped slightly last week, although the number of people out of work increased.'
The Guardian

'Today's tip tells you how to keep your hair in good condition. Cut it out and paste it on a piece of cardboard and hang it in your bathroom.'
Women's magazine

'Half-back, Brian Oxon, managed to gain three goats for his team on Saturday.'

The Sun

'The book contains a portrait of the author and several other quaint illustrations of interest to antique collectors.'

The Bookseller

'The Brass Bands' annual picnic will be hell in the country.'

Southend Standard

'A set of traffic lights has been stolen from a main road junction in Exeter. A police spokesman said: "Some thieves will stop at nothing".'

Exeter Express and Echo

'It is time the law stepped in to prohibit people who have no more sense than to make dogs follow them on bicycles, especially at night.'

Leicester Mercury

'ERRORS: No responsibility can be accepted for losses arising from typographical errors and advertisers are expected to check their smalls to ensure correct appearance.'

Rhodesia Herald

'If they could save children from dying before the age of one there was a better prospect of them reaching adulthood.'

Vermont paper

'The accident happened at Hillcrest Drive and Santa Barbara Avenue as the dead man was crossing the intersection.'

Los Angeles Times

'The Women's Institute will hold their fortnightly lecture in the Village Hall, when the topic will be "Country Life". Mrs Weeks will show slides of some beautiful wild pants.'

Matlock Mercury

'The Arrowsmith family came to South Africa when he was forty and she was twenty-seven. He was now fifty and she was twenty-nine.'

South African Weekly

'CHALLENGE! We believe that Michael Harvey, author of 1500 short stories, is the most prolific writer of all time. If any other writer, living or dead, can beat this record we would like to hear from them.'

World's Press News

'Firemen in Yorkshire received over 20 letters of thanks today thanking them for their efforts which destroyed 5 houses yesterday morning.'

Yorkshire Evening Post

'To repair damaged tablecloths, first lay the tablecloth out flat with the hole uppermost.'

Dublin Evening Mail

'Sir Robert and Lady June received many congratulations after their horse's success. The latter wore a peacock blue frock, with a pill-box hat, and matching accessories.'

Berkshire local paper

'An Arab country, like Ireland, is a place where the remarkable seldom happens, and the impossible occurs quite frequently.'

Bangladesh Times

'On their twenty-fifth wedding anniversary Mr and Mrs Walter Aston returned to the church where they were married to renew their cows.'

Crewe Chronicle

'. . . the bride's dress was gathered at the back and fell gently to the floor.'

South London paper

'The public house was a one-storey building and the occupants were sleeping on the first floor at the time of the incident.'

Welsh paper

'The winners of the competition will be flown to a first-class hotel in Florence where they will remain for two weeks without having to spend a penny.'

Sunday Mail

'The bride was wearing a gown of cream silk, and her train was at 6.30 p.m.'

Boston Post

'Many students are planning to follow the team to the scene of the bottle.'

International Herald Tribune

'"We saw over thirty deer come to the forest to feed in the early morning," said Mrs Boston, and added that they had thick sweaters and several flasks of hot tea with them.'

Dorset local paper

'Wreckage is being washed on to the beach with the tide. It is feared that there may have been a wreck.'

Scottish evening paper

'The bride was given away by her father and was held in place by a wreath of orange blossoms.'

Exeter Express

'Mrs Ponsford, infant teacher at Valley Road Primary School, was severely bitten by a dog in the school grounds. The headmistress pointed out that it might just as easily have been a child.'

Wiltshire paper

'At the lecture, Mrs Boswell gave amusing anecdotes with slides of her pet gorilla, Gertie. She said that although many ladies would be frightened of living with such a large animal, she felt completely at ease having spent 20 years in the jungle with her husband.'

Nottingham Daily Express

'The bride was very upset when one of the bridesmaids stepped on her brain and tore it.'

Bedford paper

'I am sure there will be many people who would like to see this film a second time, especially if they missed it on its first run.'

Film Weekly

'Mrs Bell wrinkled up her nose as her daughter pinned a rose on it for the photograph.'

Oxford Mail

'When washing windows, put a little vinegar in your final rinsing water. This will keep away flies as well as cleaning them.'

Woman's Weekly

'Police reported discovering a full case of champagne in a parked car last night. Sergeant Meryll said last night: "We have no clue as to whom the champagne belongs, but I have two men working on the case now."'

Connecticut paper

'Mrs Lancaster, whose husband works for British Telecom, has two other children, Barry 4½ and Sarah 9, but they are not twins.'

Mother and Baby

'The other motorist declared that Mr Dowe smelled of drink. So did a policeman.'

Daily Express

'Wooden benches for the crucial fourth India–Australia Test in Calcutta have been replaced by cricket officials.'

Reading Chronicle

'The skirt was long and pleated, and fell to her ankles where it joined a simple bodice.'

Woman's Wear Daily

'It was whilst walking home one very cold and frosty morning after an all-night party that she caught a child and died.'

Idaho paper

'During the past few days 18 bicycles have been stolen from Cambridge streets. Police feel a bicycle thief must be at work.'

Cambridge Herald

'The council is cutting down on unnecessary postage expenditure by asking householders to collect their rates bill. They will be writing to every householder to inform them of this fact.'

Bristol Evening News

'The boy was described as lazy and insolent, and when asked by his mother to go to school he threatened to "smash her brains out". The case has been adjourned for three weeks to give the boy another chance.'

The Daily Telegraph

'Princess Margaret, wearing a summery yellow-ribbed cotton dress, white brimmed hat covered with daisies and yellow sandals, was shown around the laboratories.'

Bradford Telegraph & Argus

'Sprinkle on your shelves a mixture of borax and sugar, and this will poison every aunt that finds it.'

Accrington Gazette

'Experts know that the alcoholic process takes longer in the men, but the end reshult is the same.'

Evening Standard

'The Head of the Borough Council stated that the new road would go through the centre of the cemetery, provided permission is obtained from the various bodies concerned.'

Avon Advertiser

'We note with regret that Mr Jaspar Honniton is recovering after a serious car accident.'

Moulsham Residents' Magazine

'Following the armed robbery, Police searched the house from room to room looking for gnus.'

Daily Mirror

'Strikebound holidaymakers were kept waiting over 8 hours for the jerry on Bank Holiday Monday. When it did arrive it was filled to capacity.'

Folkestone local paper

'. . . and after the Queen Mother had broken the traditional bottle of champagne on the bows of the ship, she slid gently into the water with hardly a splash, amid resounding cheers of joy from the crowd.'

Portsmouth Herald

'A tip for stretching a tight hat is to damp the head with steam from a boiling kettle.'

Oldham Evening Chronicle

'Wrap poison bottles in sandpaper and fasten with Sellotape or a rubber band. If you have children, then lock them away in a metal box.'

South Wales Echo

'The men formed a chain and tried to light the fire with buckets of water.'

Mona's Herald

'The new hospital extension will enable patients to be prepared and served in such a way that has previously been impossible.'

Toronto Daily Star

'It is small wonder that morale is low. Dentists inadequately paid for their work are said to be pulling out in droves.'

The Practitioner

'On several occasions Mr Borodin tried to get the 200-year-old violin back, but Miss Framm clained that the violin was a gift to her with no strings attached.'

Evening Standard

'Walter and I are like blood brothers. He means more to me than my own flesh and Mrs Doreen Buerk of Nickelby Road, Aldershot.'

Evening News

'The new automatic couplings fitted to the organ will enable the organist, Madge Brewer, to change her combinations without moving her feet.'

East Anglian Daily Times

'A quantity of drugs were discovered by a sniffer dog hidden in a cigarette packet.'

The Times

'Mrs Monica Rowe gave a very interesting talk on Spain, including a description of a bullfight at the Waterlooville Ladies Club last Thursday.'

Southsea Evening News

'Blend sugar, flour, and salt. Add egg and milk, cook until creamy in double boiler. Stir frequently. Add remaining ingredients. Mix well and serve chilled in individual dishes. Funeral service will be held Tuesday afternoon at two o'clock.'

Reedsburg Post

'We apologise for the error in last week's paper in which we stated that Mr Arnold Dogbury was a defective in the police force. We meant, of course, that Mr Dogbury is a detective in the police farce, and are sorry for any embarrassment caused.'

Cape Times

'Because elderly people find it difficult to climb the hill, the District Council have agreed to put a seat at the top.'

North Somerset Mercury

'A tornedo swept over New York last night killing 8 people and doing damage to humorous buildings.'

American paper

'Already disqualified from driving for life, 32-year-old George Henderson, unemployed, was disqualified for a further five years at Liverpool Crown Court yesterday.'

Liverpool Echo

'Mr Hawkins planned and built the bungalow himself from books borrowed from the local library.'

Jersey paper

'Later that afternoon she discovered the cat dead in the garden, and curried its body indoors.'

Wolverhampton Express & Star

3 'Rest in peace until we meet again'

We live and learn. Then, of course, we die and forget all, but our mistakes are often remembered long after we are gone. Here are some grave errors that have been made on tombstones; mistakes that will be remembered forever.

Sacred to the memory of
MAJOR JAMES BRUSH
Who was killed by
the
accidental discharge
of a pistol by
his orderly on the
14th April Eighteen Eighty Three
'Well done thou good and
faithful servant.'

Here lies the body of JOHN MOUND
Who was lost at sea and never found.

Here lie the remains of THOMAS NICOLLS
Who died in Philadelphia, March 1578.
Had he lived he would have been buried here.

Richard Kendrick
Was buried here on
August 29th 1785
by the desire of his wife
Margaret Kendrick.

Here lies the body of
A BURGLAR
Shot whilst robbing a store.
This stone was
Erected with money found
on him.

Alice Mary Johnson 1883–1947
Let her RIP.

Here lies the body of THOMAS VERNON
The only surviving son of Admiral Vernon.
Died 23rd July 1753.

Erected to the memory of
JOHN MacFARLANE
Drowned in the waters of Leith
By a few affectionate friends.

Here lies returned to clay
Miss Arabella Young
Who on the first of May
Began to hold her tongue.

Here lies the body of
SAMUEL YOUNG
Who came here and died
for the benefit of his health.

This gallant young man
gave up his life
in the attempt
to save a perishing lady.

In memory of
JOHN SMITH
Who met weirlent death neer this
spot 18 hundred 40 too.
He was shot by his own pistol.
It was not one of the new kind
but an old fashioned brass barrel
and of such is the
KINGDOM OF HEAVEN

Here lies
Father and Mother and Sister and I.
We all died within the space of one year.
They all be buried at Wimble, except I
And I be buried here.

The last laugh . . .

'We have to inform you of the sad death of Mr Giddings, recalled to God by accident.'

Glasgow newspaper

'It would be a great help towards keeping the churchyard in good order if everyone would follow the example of those that clip the grass on their own grave.'

Parish magazine

'Mr Morris died in New Plymouth Hospital last night. His condition is said to be as well as can be expected.'

Torbay News

'POSKINS – to the memory of Mr Isaac Poskins, passed away June 8. Peace at last. From all the neighbours of Winfield Road.'

Sheffield Star

'In loving memory of a dear husband and dad. Passed over September 18. Always in our thoughts. Will accept £50 or nearest offer, no dealers. Write Box 29.675.'

Dorset paper

'The Rev Aldus will no longer be able to attend the meeting on Friday, owing to his recent death.'

Coventry paper

'On August 11, Mr Bryant suffered a stroke but with the loving care of his family and nurse he never fully recovered.'

Australian paper

'A woman mourner was horrified when her best hat was buried with the coffin at a South African funeral – it was mistaken for a floral wreath. She had intended to wear it the following evening at a cocktail party.'

Weekend Mail

Not so dead

François de Civille was pronounced dead in 1562 and was duly buried. Six hours after the funeral his brother had an intuition that François was still alive and promptly went along to the cemetery and had him dug up again. The 'corpse' revived and lived seventy years longer, dying at the age of 105 as the result of a cold, caught whilst serenading his sweetheart all night long!

In Ontario, Canada, it was a sad day for friends and relatives of Mrs Sadie Tuckey. She had been accidentally knocked off her bicycle and killed. When the funeral was held, scores of mourners came to pay their last respects, but as the coffin was being carried to its final resting place the mourners themselves nearly died of shock when they saw the 'body' sit up in the coffin. Sadie was not dead at all! She had merely been stunned into a deep coma. The 'body' screamed, leapt out of the coffin with fright and ran down the road, straight into the path of a bus and was killed outright.

Last will and testament

Always be kind to animals. In 1917 a wealthy Austrian woman, Mathilde Kovacs, burned her entire fortune just before her death – because her family had been unkind to her cats and she did not want them to enjoy her money.

In September 1944, a Brooklyn lawyer left over £25 000 to his cat, thereby cutting out five relatives because they disliked his favourite pet.

Don't make the mistake of believing the dead won't have the last laugh. Here is what Mary David heard at the reading of the will of David Davis, who died in 1788:

'I, David Davis, of Clapham, Surrey, do give and bequeath to Mary David, daughter of Peter Delaport, the sum of five shillings, sufficient for her to get drunk for the last time at my expense.'

4 'I've only got two pairs of hands'

Long, long ago a very wise philosopher named Zeno of Citium said: 'It is better to trip with the feet than the tongue. If you slip over you can soon put a bandage on your cut knee, but nothing can cover up your blushes when you have a slip of the tongue!' The following slips caused some very red faces! What they actually said wasn't quite what they intended.

'Alice has always been lucky. Even the sun was shining when she first saw it.'

'I have felt very ill all night and it has left me with a very bad head. I hope to shake it off today.'

'Fry the baby while I feed the sausages, will you?'

'During the last war we were evaporated to the country.'

'We went to the aquarium at Brighton and watched the delphiniums jump through hoops.'

'His car is a white, "S" registration, hunchback.'

'If the baby does not thrive on raw milk, boil it.'

'Oh look, a lorry's hijacked and we'll have to pass by on the cold shoulder.'

'Well, nobody's inflammable you know. . . .'

'I apologise for biting your heads off just now.'

'Practise the art of deep breathing. Take a deep breath, hold it as long as you can and then expire.'

'Now, if you don't come back, I shan't let you go again.'

'I got something off my chest today that's been hanging over my head for some time. That's behind me now, thank goodness.'

'Rain was coming down the walls like water.'

'If you put two and two together then the cat comes out of the bag.'

'For those of you who have small children and don't know it, we have a play area outside.'

'She was so happy that tears rose to her lips.'

'My husband communicates to London every day on the train.'

'Just what are you incinerating?'

'I was so surprised you could have knocked me down with a fender.'

'Mrs Godfrey can make sponge cakes as light and fluffy as any of my friends.'

'We must keep our ears to the ground if we want to keep our heads above water.'

'Even more astonishing was our saving the lives of little babies who formerly died from sheer ignorance.'

'I count the trees on the wallpaper to get to sleep at night. I always sleep like a log.'

'All of this ice is frozen.'

'He spent the early part of his life on the back of a horse with a pipe in his mouth.'

'Mr Selwyn Lloyd has plans to break this oil bottleneck up his sleeve.'

'Apples don't grow on trees, you know.'

'They still use inches to measure horses' hands.'

'. . . and remember, you can make a very nourishing soup from the remains if you have an invalid in the house.'

'In Germany a person cannot slaughter any animal without being rendered unconscious first.'

'In 1675 Frederick William defeated a Swedish army twice his size.'

'A gentleman never crumbles his bread or rolls in his soup.'

'Will you lend me a rifle so I can shoot myself?'

'We were able to see right into the Royal disclosure.'

'That's the most illegible excuse I've ever heard.'

'The knife slipped and she cut herself severely in the pantry.'

'In England this happens one hundred times out of a hundred – that's nearly always.'

'Watch with one eye and listen with the other.'

'If you wish to talk, ask me first.'

'The four points make an equilateral triangle.'

'Your head looks just like my husband's behind.'

'This is a compulsory part of the exam and you have to take it.'

'My sister uses massacre on her eyes.'

'I can't blame you for wanting to go outside and sit on your ten minute break.'

'Do you remember when we used to play cowboys and Indians, you were my brave and I was your squawk?'

'Man is a very efficient machine.'

'When the water reaches 25°C, take the temperature.'

'In one word – I don't think so.'

'Every director bites the hand that lays the golden egg.'

'My father is retarded on a pension.'

'I read part of the book all the way through.'

'If my mother was alive she'd turn over in her grave.'

'The food was delivered to over 100 senior citizens living locally in a wheelbarrow.'

'Save time and cut fingers with an electric carving knife.'

'Nothing he says is worth the paper it's written on.'

'Anybody who goes to see a psychiatrist ought to have his head examined.'

'We're going to make some thermostat copies of this letter so that everybody can have one.'

'I can't tell what the weather's like – it's too foggy to see.'

'Don't let the dog hang out of the car window whilst driving.'

'A dog will not bite your hand or wag its tail unless it likes you.'

'His mother lived to be nearly a centurion.'

'This is a very serious offence which we have to deal with severely, as a detergent to anyone else.'

'I am all for a bit of fun, boys, but when it comes to scattering tintacks on the changing-room floor, I really must put my foot down.'

'I had tremendous fun chasing a rabbit on a motorbike, but I couldn't catch it.'

'Without a word of warning the cows ran across the road.'

'If you can't give me your word of honour, will you give me your promise?'

'There have been a number of fatalities recently, but no serious accidents.'

'Let us nip this political monkey in the bud before it sticks to us like a leech.'

'Every time I open my mouth some idiot starts talking.'

'Many gardeners are suffering from greenfly this year.'

'I'll give you a definite maybe.'

'She was declining flat out on a sofa.'

'My doctor gave me a conscription for some medicine.'

'A bachelor's life is no life for a single man.'

Spoonerisms

In history, one person stands out above all others for making the most slips of the tongue and he is the Reverend William Archibald Spooner. He is famous for muddling up the first letters of his words, so that when he tried to say 'cherry pie' it would come out as 'perry chie'! His mistakes are so well-known that he has actually given his name to a word in the English language – such a slip is now known as a spoonerism. Here are some of his best known spoonerisms. Whether or not he actually said them all we shall never know, but we like to think so!

'You have hissed all my mystery lectures.'

'Give me a well-boiled icycle.'

'You will leave on the next town drain.'

'Kinquering Congs their titles take.'

'Let us drink to the queer old Dean.'

'You will find as you grow older that the weight of rages will press harder and harder on the employer.'

'I have in my breast a half-warmed fish.'

'You have been caught fighting a liar in the quad.'

'Sir, you have tasted two whole worms.'

'I have frost a very dear lend.'

5 'The best is none too good'

The English language is very difficult. Especially if you happen to be foreign! English people never learn foreign languages themselves because they know that all foreigners have to learn English, and when the Englishman goes abroad he expects everything to be translated for him. When you consider that we 'water a horse' but we don't 'milk a cat', and the fact that so many words sound exactly the same, then it's not surprising that foreigners can have just a little difficulty with translation.

An advertisement in a Belgian forwarding office:

Hand your baggage to us – we will send it in all directions.

Notice in an Austrian hotel:

In case of fire please do your utmost to alarm the hall porter.

From a bulb catalogue bought in Holland:

It is the hyacinth which in the past has laid the lion's share of golden eggs for the Dutch nurserymen.

Seen in a catalogue at an Italian museum:

Attention must draw to a collection of local beetles – modestly encased in drawers, but one wonders at the exhibition.

Advertisement in a Spanish newspaper:
Engliss shorthanded typist. Efficien. Useless. Apply otherwise.

Sign in Brazilian hotel:
Touch not switch wire you in for a shock otherwise.

Notice in Cyprus restaurant:
After the typhoid academic, customers are assured that all vegetables are boiled in water passed by the manager.

Seen outside a French restaurant:
RESTAURANT SUR LA MER
Aujourd'hui . . . L'Iris stew.

Sign in Italy:
To relive traffic digestion, take Astorio ferry every fifteen minutes.

From a guidebook about Malta:
Although every care has been taken, us do not accept responsibility for inoccuracies.

From a Cyprus newspaper:
. . . modern new atom-power station with unique giant sphere 135 ft across built to house vicar.

Notice in a Spanish hotel:
It is forbidded to steal hotel towns. If you are person not to do such is please not to read this notice.

Advert for a Nigerian bus company:
The comfort in our buses is next to none.

From an East African paper:

In Nairobi there are few things more hereditary than swine mouths and under-shot, also soft and fluffy coats.

A leaflet printed in Venice enquires:

DO YOU WANT TO CHANGE IN VENICE?
Change at the Savings Bank.

From a French newspaper:

Le Capitaine Miller, en uniforme des Cold Cream Guards.

Notice in an Austrian hotel:

Visitors are requested not to throw coffee or other matter into the basin. Why else it stuffs the place inconvenient for the other world.

Notice in a Bulgarian hotel:

If you are satisfactory, tell all your friend.
If you are unsatisfactory, warn the waitress.

Driving instructions from Germany:

At a police controlled crossing, drivers who wish to turn right should wait for the all clear before running over the policeman.

Bedroom notice in an Italian hotel:

Do not adjust your light hanger. See the manager if you need more light.

Instructions in a Spanish lift:

To move the cabin, push button of wishing floor. If the cabin should enter more persons, each person should press number of wishing floor. Driving is then going alphabetically by natural order. Button retaining pressed position shows received command for visiting station.

Notice to guests in a French hotel:

In the event of fire, the visitor, avoiding panic is to walk down the corridor and warm the chambermaid.

Sign by swimming pool in Majorca:

Bathers are reminded that they must be fully dressed on entry into the swimming pools and must be fully dressed on leaving the swimming pools.

Handbill from the Pamplona festival (northern Spain):
WHAT YOU MUST NOT DO
To walk around alone in groups or in an inadequate form, and adopting attitudes that denote a confidential bad state to offend the elemental conduct.

To make noises and scandlas in the sight of the public and establishments.

Sit down or lie down in the sight of the people to obstruct the freedom of the public.

To utilise percusion instruments after midnight or tear objects in the crowded private places.

Sign in Germany:

Warning: if river bunk flows depart water instant.

Washing instructions with socks:

The manufacturers of this hose must be washed in luke warm water, never hot and remove soap from water.

From a Spanish newspaper:

Recent animals included Mr and Mrs Ellis.

Instructions on a foreign food packet:

To do what: Besmear a backing pan, previously buttered with a good tomato sauce and after, dispose Canelloni, lightly distanced between them in a only couch.

48

Guide book to a Swiss holiday resort explains:

This is the best resort for anyone who wants peace and solitude. Millions flock here from all over the world in search of such quiet.

Sign in an Egyptian hotel:

If you require room service, leave room and shout 'Room service' at porter.

Advertisement in a Brazilian newspaper:

Paying guest. Goog opporuny for a snigla refined gentleman. Large room, nicely furnished, splendidd food. Six sindoros facing sea, quite close to blushing beach.

Notice on an Italian camp site:

By order of police, one obliges the frequenters of the Camping to are wearing bathing costumes that are not giving offence to the morals.

Notice in a village café in France:

Persons are requested not to occupy seats in this café if they wish not to consume them.

From restaurants around the world the following dishes have appeared:

Hand and eeg
Frightened eegs
Sauceage eeg an chaps
Battered cod peaces

Bruined squid
Baked cheese fingers
Spitted haddock fish

Soap of the day
Hard eeg with source mayonnaise
Hen soop
Spaghetti fungus
Staited calamary
Red mallet

Roped carrots
Rise
Liver offal with stuffed

Marooned Duchess with steak surprise
Two peasants
Larks in the spit
Angry duck in orange sorts

'Enjoy to eat now – always bring back later'
Local mutto.

*If you found it difficult to choose from that menu, try this
one from a luxury hotel in Cairo:*

Fizz Soup
Boled eegs in creme sorse
Muscles of Marines
Frog leagues

Lioness cutlet
Tongue leaf with leaves
Venison Parcel
Surprised chicken
Cracked Tarts
Rice hashed
Mucked shrimp

Speciality of the hows: Young Dear Hunter
(Flush of young dear, objerjeans, muchrooms end
spaces, in white whine sorts, all cooked up in your
seat.)

Yogrot and gropes
Eyes creme
Jum Dognuts
Biscuit cease
Pankasises
Pankasies with bebber and jem
Apple crumbs
Live fruit
Rhubarb and prune shock

We recommend the cheez of the neighbours
Coughee Eggspress
Service not comprehended

If you wish to show your feelings then wait untill
you see the manageress

Notice in foyer of a Japanese hotel:

Sports jackets may be worn, but never trousers.

From a guidebook about Sardinia:

To remember of this period are the failed landing of the
French revolutionaries on the northern coast of the island
(1793), the uprising (1795), the consequent march of the
judge C. M. Angioi on Cagliari, thwarted off at Oristano in
1796 and the attempt also fruitless of the notary Cilocca.

Even trained interpreters can make mistakes. The phrase
'Out of sight, out of mind' was translated into Russian and
then back into English as 'Invisible lunatic', and a Chinese
interpreter translated the slogan 'Come alive with Pepsi' as
'Pepsi brings your relatives back from the dead'! Well, we
all make mistakes. . . .

6 'Bamboo is a Disney cartoon fawn'

We learn from our mistakes. At least that's what we are told, and if the following howlers culled from classrooms all over the country are anything to go by, then we have a lot of budding geniuses on our hands. Here are some classic clangers.

'A polar bear is a nude Eskimo.'

'A parole is a special kind of bun they eat in prisons.'

'Doggerel is a little puppy with a short tail and several pauses.'

'Jacob had a brother called See-Saw.'

'In France even pheasants drink wine.'

'Shakespeare wrote tragedy, comedy and errors.'

'My sister has an allegory. If she eats strawberries she comes out in a rash.'

'King Solomon had a thousand wives and a lot of conquered turbines.'

'Reefs are what you put on coffins.'

'Henry VIII had an abbess on each knee and could not walk.'

'Rabies are Jewish priests that have to be quarantined for six months.'

'A plumber is a man who picks plums for a living.'

'Irrigation is when you have to scratch it.'

'When a dog has puppies it's called a litre.'

'Chaplets are little churches.'

'Gretna Green is a poison for killing rats.'

'Aspiring is something you take for headaches.'

'Doctors practise medicine until they get it right.'

'Florence Nightingale used to sing in Berkeley Square.'

'An Indian baby is called a caboose.'

'A mosquito is a black child of white parents.'

'A virgin forest is a place where the hand of man has never set foot.'

'Nuclear power stations are built in places on the coast such as Luton.'

'An oxygen has eight sides.'

'Cleopatra died from the bite of a wasp.'

'An apiary is where a zoo keeps its monkeys.'

'So Henry VIII with the help of Cromwell set about dissolutioning the monasteries.'

'Nelson commanded the Victory and died on a plaque which marks a spot on the sea where he fell.'

'The mayonnaise is the French national anthem.'

'A centurion is a Roman who is a hundred years old.'

'Coal-fire power stations should be built in the minefields.'

'Napoleon had three children, none of which lived to maternity.'

'Handel was a little boy in a book by Grimm. He had a sister called Gristle.'

'We get lead pencils from petrified trees.'

'There are many types of eligible fish in the sea.'

'A fjord is a Norwegian car.'

'The masculine of vixen is vicar.'

'Monsoon is a French word meaning Mister.'

'The future of "I give" is "you take".'

'A hostage is a nice lady on an aeroplane.'

'Marconi invented the radio.'

'Our cat has fleas so it keeps on etching.'

'Conservation is when you talk to people.'

'Autobiography is the history of motorcars.'

'Margarine is made from imitation cows.'

'Ambiguity is telling the truth when you don't mean it.'

'The smallest wind instrument is the Piccadilly.'

'A spatula is a bone behind your shoulderblade.'

'Flora and Fauna are two Siamese twins.'

'A fencer is someone who puts up fences.'

'The liver is an infernal organ.'

'The robbers held up the bank and got away with the lute.'

'Moths eat hardly nothing, except holes.'

'Manilla is a city famous for its envelopes.'

'Late invoices are things you hear in a haunted house.'

'Income is a yearly tax.'

'Soviet is another name for a table napkin.'

'Belvedere is the name of a male deer.'

'The Navy is sometimes called the senile service.'

'Magnets are little creatures found in rotten apples.'

'Atlas carried the world on his head and later made maps with it.'

'Vandals are open-toed shoes worn by the ancient Romans.'

'Washington was a great general, he always had a fixed determination to win or lose.'

'Flotsam and Jetsam were a team of coloured comedians.'

'The Conga river is in Africa.'

'The modern era is the mistakes being made today.'

'It is sometimes difficult to hear what is being said in church because the agnostics are so bad.'

'Homer wrote a play called the Oddity.'

'The bowels are a, e, i, o, u and sometimes w and y.'

'The king knighted the hero with his royal spectre.'

'Monotony means when a man has only one wife.'

56

'Poetry is when every line starts with a capital letter.'

'Livid was a famous Roman poet.'

'A Papal bull is a male cow owned by the Pope.'

'A mongoose is a male French duck.'

'A medicine ball is a dance for sick people.'

'Boxers sometimes give each other a paunch on the nose.'

'The mother of Abraham Lincoln died in infancy.'

'Mata Hari means Japanese suicide.'

'If you try to cut through atoms they split.'

'An executive is a man who chops people's heads off.'

'The Gorgons had long snakes in their hair and looked like women only more horrible.'

'The natives of Macedonia did not believe, so St Paul got stoned.'

'Blood consists of red and white corkscrews.'

'A blizzard is the inside of a chicken.'

'A hippie is a tiny little hippo.'

'Socrates died from an overdose of wedlock.'

'Saint Peter was a rabbit in a book by Beatrice Potter.'

'Tadpoles eat one another until they become frogs.'

'LXX stands for love and kisses.'

'*An optimist is a man who makes spectacles.*'

'A curve is the longest line between two points.'

'*My mother is in the Middle Ages.*'

'Karl Marx was the Marx brother who played a harp.'

'*Taxes is a place with a lot of cowboys.*'

'A centimetre is an insect with a hundred legs.'

'*Philatelists were a race of people who lived in Biblical times.*'

'A priory means first come first served.'

'*Pot-pourri is a French dish served in hot little pots.*'

'Tunisia is a disease where you lose your memory.'

'*Gravity is that which if there was none we would all fly away.*'

'Clive committed suicide three times.'

'*Dusk is little bits of fluff found under the bed.*'

'A marionette is a net in which fishermen catch little fish known as marions.'

'*Africa is separated from Europe by the Sewage Canal, which Disraeli dug out for Queen Victoria.*'

'Pegasus is a hobby horse used by carpenters.'

'*Insects is burnt in churches.*'

'The horizon is a line where the land meets the sky but isn't there when you get there.'

'On the back of buses no smoking is aloud.'

'Offa's Dyke was a church. Offa was a rather irrelevant king.'

'Venison is a city in Italy with a lot of canals.'

'Geranium is used to make atom bombs.'

'A baboon is a musical instruments blown in bands.'

'We had some salad for launch today.'

'King Arthur, if he existed, would have been noble, brave, and probably a little potty.'

'Alligator shoes are made from crocodile skin.'

'Vergil was a man who worked in a church.'

'Heat moves through water with conviction.'

'An epistle is the wife of an apostle.'

'People who live in Paris are called Parisites.'

'Ruby Tanyer is a song about the sea.'

'An average is something it rains on.'

'The wife of a duke is a ducky.'

'Noah's wife was Joan of Arc.'

'A widow is a wife without a man.'

'A surefooted animal is one that when it kicks it does not miss.'

'Atomic weights are used for weighing atoms.'

'If you squeeze the juice out of mud you get dust.'

'Wolsey saved his life by dying before he got to London.'

'The second wife of Henry VIII was Ann Berlin.'

'Herrings swim about the sea in shawls.'

'The first commandment was when Eve told Adam to eat the apple.'

'Telepathy is a code invented by Morse.'

'An antibody is someone who doesn't like nudist camps.'

'People living on the Equator are called equations.'

'Augustus remained in the same position for four years.'

'The Spanish Armada had to wait whilst Drake finished his game of bowels.'

'An epitaph is a short sarcastic poem.'

'Faith is believing what you know to be untrue.'

'During the war crowned heads of Europe were trembling in their shoes.'

'Poetry is a thing you make prose of.'

'Polonius was a sort of sausage.'

'Skyscrapers are a sort of telescope.'

'The Diet of Worms was an old-fashioned recipe for slimmers.'

'Beau Brummel was a well-dressed dandy from Birmingham.'

'A monologue is a dialogue by one person.'

'People go to Africa to hunt rhinostriches.'

'A cuckoo is a bird what lays other birds' eggs in its nest.'

'Pineapples grow on pine trees.'

'A buttress is a female butcher.'

'Alias was a man in the bible.'

'Palsy is a vicar in Northern Ireland.'

'Tarzan is another name for the American flag – Tarzan stripes.'

'Another name for vinegar is gaul.'

'Electric volts are named after Voltaire who invented electricity.'

'A polygon is another name for a Mormon.'

'Garibaldi designed the Statue of Liberty.'

'The Moaner Liza is a picture famous for her smile.'

'The earth resolves around the sun once a year.'

'A ruminating animal chews its cubs.'

'In America some murderers are put to death by electrolysis.'

'El Giza is the name of a Spanish water heater.'

'The Pied Piper told the mayor he could get rid of all the rates.'

'Marshal Goering was a fat man and one of Hitler's stoutest supporters.'

'The silk used to make ladies' underwear is called Crepe Suzette.'

'The Colossus of Rhodes is Spaghetti Junction.'

'The Normans put mokes around their forts.'

'He was persecuted for taking brides.'

'Catholics believe what the Pope tells them but protestants believe what they like.'

'Infra dig means living in lodgings.'

'Most of Falmouth's small peninsula is covered with water at all times, except the small section of the harbour.'

'Pidgin-English is what pigeons used to carry messages during the war.'

'Opium is a drug invented by Dr Fu Manchu.'

'Mercury was an Ancient Greek god and can now be found inside a thermometer.'

'A conservative is like a glass porch on a house.'

'Near the corpse stood the old cottage.'

'To get pills you need a doctor's postscript.'

'The plural of spouse is spice.'

'Armadillo is the Spanish navy defeated by the Duke of Wellington.'

'Zero was a Roman king who fiddled while Rome burned.'

'Nicotine is the man who invented cigarettes.'

'A palmist is someone who tells your fortune by looking in a crystal ball.'

'Naval stores is where sailors' wives go shopping.'

'Cattle and pigs are bought on the stock market.'

'Newton discovered gravity when an apple fell out of a tree and struck him as being curious.'

'Vikings had horns growing out of their heads and were called great Danes.'

'A line is a length with no breath.'

'Etiquette is the noise you make when you sneeze.'

'Waltz time is sometimes called cripple time.'

'Cow hide is used for making suitcases and covering cows.'

'Sir Walter Rally bought tobaco from a man called Nick O'Teen and rolled up cigarettes with it.'

'People who live in Moscow are called mosquitoes.'

7 'Spaghetti comes from China'

Are you strong enough to face facts? We like to believe that Cleopatra died from the bite of an asp, that Cinderella wore a glass slipper, and that the Emperor Nero played the fiddle whilst Rome burned down. Sadly none of these 'events' really happened, they are all pure fallacy. If you don't want to have your illusions shattered then skip this section of the book. If you want to know the truth, then read on.

Snakes are not slimy as many people believe. If you have ever touched one you will know that a snake's skin is perfectly dry.

Chop suey is not a Chinese dish. It actually originated in California.

If you were asked to name a typical Italian food, probably the first thing you would say would be spaghetti, and you would be wrong! Spaghetti was originally eaten in China and only reached Italy in the Middle Ages.

We all know the story of Cinderella and her beautiful glass slippers; how she won the love of Prince Charming at the ball and eventually married him – all because the glass slipper she left behind at the ball enabled him to find her again. Not so many people know that the original Cinderella did not wear glass slippers at all, but fur slippers.

So how did this mistake come about? It happened nearly three hundred years ago when the story, which was originally written in French, was translated into English. In the original the author, Charles Perrault, said that Cinders wore 'pantoufles en vair' but the translator mistook the word vair which means fur for the word verre which means glass. So, since that day Cinderella has worn glass slippers!

Whenever we talk of ostriches we always think of them as being very timid creatures, burying their heads in the sand when they are frightened. Ostriches can, however, be very fierce and it is never wise to get too close to them. The only time they have their heads in the sand is when they are searching for food, or burying their eggs for protection.

There are thirty-five more kilometres of canal in Birmingham than there are in Venice, although we always think of Venice as having more canals than anywhere else in the world. Probably because it is a much more beautiful city than Birmingham!

Marie Antoinette did not say 'Let them eat cake'. This story was put about by people in opposition to her husband, King Lous·XVI of France. It was supposed to show how little she cared that the ordinary people of France were starving and had no bread. The phrase actually appeared in a novel over thirty years before.

It is pure fallacy that the nightingale only sings at night – it sings during the day as well.

There is no real reason for baiting a mousetrap with cheese. Mice like all kinds of food and there is no proof that they have any special preference for cheese.

Catgut does not come from cats, it comes from sheep.

One of the most famous legends of all time must be that of Cleopatra's death. Ever since the time this famous queen of Egypt died in 30 BC it has been thought that she committed suicide by clasping an asp to her bosom. This theory was brought about because the Roman general Octavian rode in triumph through the streets of Rome, followed by a chariot containing a figure of the dead Cleopatra on a couch. Entwined around this figure was the model of an asp. In reality, Cleopatra had a hollow bodkin containing poison that she pushed into her left arm.

When you are lying on the beach in the hot sun it is very tempting to have an ice cream or an ice lolly to cool you down. But in fact you'd be better with a hot cup of tea! The tea would make you sweat, and the evaporation of the moisture on your skin would cool you down.

The Belgian hare is not a hare, it is a rabbit.

It is a mistake to say that the moon shines. It doesn't. It has no light of its own and only reflects the light of the sun.

There is no soda in soda water. Like other sparkling drinks it is charged with carbon dioxide.

On the Embankment in London there is an obelisk known as Cleopatra's needle. It has no connection with Cleopatra and was one of two erected in Egypt over 1000 years before she was even born.

The sky is not blue. It is colourless. The colour we see is caused by the scattering of the sun's rays, caused by dust in the Earth's atmosphere.

Great Dane dogs come from Germany and have nothing to do with Denmark.

Indian ink actually comes from China.

The 'goose-step' which we always associate with German soldiers is a British invention. It was introduced by the

British Army as a method of seeing whether or not any of the soldiers were drunk.

Little Miss Muffet is not just the subject of a nursery rhyme as you might believe, she was a real person.

Rats do not desert a sinking ship as is popularly believed. They are not able to predict a disaster, so if a ship sinks then the rats on board go down with it.

The Emperor Nero did not fiddle while Rome burned. Fiddles had not been invented, and at the time he was 80 km away from Rome in his villa.

The Battle of Hastings in 1066 was not fought at Hastings. It was fought about 10 km away at a place which is now called Battle.

We often imagine that there are hundreds of wild animals that could eat us up, especially if we were to be walking alone through the jungle. There are, however, fewer than ten species that have the jaws or the teeth capable of eating a man.

A pythoness is a witch or female soothsayer, not a snake.

The centipede does not have a hundred legs: the most common type has about 42, although some have more than 100 *pairs*. Millipedes don't have a thousand legs either: very few have more than 200.

Baked beans are not a modern invention, they were eaten as long ago as 1830.

Have you ever heard someone say that flowers must be removed from a bedroom at night? This is because they believe flowers give off so much carbon dioxide that it is dangerous to have them in a room whilst you are sleeping. Although flowers do give off carbon dioxide at night, the amount is so small that even if you slept in a room full of blooms there would be very little difference to the oxygen content and you would be perfectly all right.

Have you heard the saying 'Like a red rag to a bull'? This saying came about because it is mistakenly believed that the colour red makes a bull angry. Wrong! Bulls are colour-blind and cannot tell red from any other colour.

If you ever get bitten by a mosquito you can in all truthfulness declare that it was a female insect that bit you. That is because male mosquitoes are vegetarians and it is only the females that bite.

Rhubarb is not a fruit, it is a vegetable.

Some people believe that all animals sit or lie down to sleep. Not at all. Horses, elephants, zebras and antelopes are among many animals that can sleep standing up.

If someone tells you that snakes can be found in every part of the British Isles – he is wrong. There are no snakes found in Ireland.

Fireflies and glow-worms are not worms or flies, they are both beetles.

Throughout the centuries, many statues and pictures of Queen Boadicea have depicted her riding a chariot with scythes on the chariot axles. It is very unlikely that she did so; first, because there is no evidence that such a weapon was used at that particular time, and second, if it was intended to chop off the legs of the Romans as she rode along, it is more than likely that her own soldiers and horses would have lost legs too.

Hair cannot naturally turn white overnight. Hair that has already grown cannot change colour, except, of course, if you dye or bleach it!

Charles Lindbergh was not the first person to fly non-stop across the Atlantic. He was the sixty-seventh! He was, nevertheless, the first person to do it alone.

Mustard gas is not a gas; nor is it a mustard. It is a liquid whose *vapour* burns the skin and causes blindness.

Snakes cannot be charmed by music because they have no ears and are deaf to music. They can, however, respond to vibration and so can feel a snake-charmer's foot tapping rather than hear his music.

King John did not sign the Magna Carta – he could not write. Instead, he showed his agreement by setting his seal to the charter.

Have you ever been told: an apple a day keeps the doctor away? This saying originated because apples contain vitamin C, but there is no real evidence that vitamin C actually prevents illness, and even if it did there are many other fruits, such as oranges, which contain a much higher percentage.

A person's last important action before they retire or die is often called their swan song, because it was thought that swans, before they die, break into a most beautiful song. However, this is completely untrue. Swans do not sing before they die; in fact they do not sing at any other time either for they are mute, apart from making the odd croaking sound.

Everybody knows the Bible story of Adam and Eve and the eating of the apple – or do they? Nowhere in the whole Bible is there mention of an apple. In the Book of Genesis Adam and Eve ate the 'forbidden fruit', but we are never told that the fruit was actually an apple.

Most of the things we taste, or that we actually call tastes, are smells.

Buffalo Bill hunted bison, not buffalo!

The silk worm is not a worm, but the larva of a moth.

The primrose is not a rose. It is so called because it flowers in spring; the 'prim' part of the word is from the Latin 'prima' meaning first.

The North Pole is usually considered to be the coldest place on earth, but the coldest temperatures ever recorded have been in Verkhoyansk in northern Siberia where it has been minus 90° fahrenheit (minus 68° centigrade).

Wormwood is not a wood, neither is it a worm. It is an aromatic plant.

Camel hair brushes are not made from camels' hair, but from the tail hairs of squirrels.

Concrete is by no means a recent invention. The Romans used it thousands of years ago.

Buttermilk does not contain any butter at all. It is the liquid left behind after the butter has been separated from milk.

Turkish baths were devised by the Romans, not the Turks.

Do you believe that you should 'feed a cold and starve a fever'? You do? Well, you're wrong. It is a popular belief but there is not a shred of medical evidence to prove it. Whether you have a cold or a fever you are better off eating your normal diet if you can. If you eat too much you will put on weight, which is bad for you. If you eat too little you will have very little energy and it will take much longer to get better.

Shooting stars are not stars but meteors.

The chalk that school teachers use to write on blackboards is not really chalk at all, it is made from plaster of paris.

A pineapple is neither pine nor apple – it is a berry.

A potato is not a fruit or a vegetable – it is a tuber, or fleshy underground stem.

A chameleon is noted for its ability to change colour to suit it surroundings, but it is fear, and changes in light and temperature, that cause the colour change – not sensitivity to the colour of its surroundings.

8 'God roves in a mysterious day'

Nobody is perfect. Not even clergymen can avoid making errors, and there are times when they drop the most unholy clangers imaginable. One Reverend Yeomens decided that the hymn 'I cannot help but wonder where I'm bound' was being sung much too slowly and mournfully, so he decided to liven it up by dancing down the aisle. Halfway down the aisle, the floorboards, unused to such enthusiastic worship, gave way under him and the startled vicar shot down into the central heating boiler! There are times when even the Pope would have to smile.

From a parish magazine:

The Reverend Oscar Mullins will begin his annual holiday on September 22. He requests that all missionary boxes be returned to him no later than September 20.

From a church newsletter:

Again the problem has arisen as to how we can get young people to join the church and stick with us, and as usual we ask for adhesive stamps.

Seen outside a small chapel in Gwent:

DON'T LET WORRY KILL YOU OFF – LET THE CHURCH HELP.

A vicar announced in his parish magazine:

Prebendary Brinsley-Smythe will be preaching at St Margaret's on Sunday 14 May, and my colleague the Right Reverend Arnold Dean on Sunday 21 May. On both these Sundays I hope to be away in Scotland.

From a church festival review:

To relieve the boredom of sitting for such long periods, the congregation were asked to stand and sing: 'Fixed in His everlasting seat'.

Seen in an American newspaper:

The Reverend Norbert Honker has spoken in all the large churches in America. To miss hearing him would be the chance of a lifetime.

The bishop wrote to his various parishes:

Will parishes who have so far made no payment please do so before the end of the month and so save my grey hairs. There are 32 of them at the present time.

Searching problem:

For ten years the vicar of St Luke's was puzzled by a simple stone slab in his church which bore the initials H.W.P. He searched all the parish registers to discover whom the initials referred to, hoping that it was some great personage. Eventually the local plumber solved the problem – the initials stood for Hot Water Pipe.

From a church newsletter:

At the end of the service the choir will sing the anthem 'Come Let Us Fall', which has been especially composed by Miss Bloomswell, the organist, after which the church will be closed for the necessary repairs.

From a parish newsletter in Birmingham:

In the Church Hall on Sunday at 6.30 p.m.: THE DEVIL.

From a letter by an angry bishop to a newspaper:

Your correspondent is wrong to suggest that the Church only supports the rich people. To the true Christian there is no class distinction – everyone is equal. What your report says is a typical attitude of the Working Classes.

From an obituary:

Soon after the Reverend Barnett came to the church a series of national disasters took place, starting with the burning of the Crystal Palace and ending with the outbreak of war.

From an Oxford paper:

The Reverend Jones has had a striking career. He started life at the age of eleven. . . .

Announcement in a parish magazine:

Miss Vokes, the editor, wishes to thank the vicar for his kind help in editing this issue whilst she was on holiday, and apologises for any shortcomings as a result.

The Reverend Edgar Dodson of Campden chose as his theme for his sermon one Sunday the commandment 'Thou Shalt Not Steal'. During the service someone stole his car from outside the church.

From the order of service, St Jude's, Ramsgate:

> *Hymn:* number 483
> (congregation standing)
> *Sermon:* What Are You Standing For?

From a Welsh newspaper:

The Right Reverend Hugh Ponsford, ugly and unsightly heap of rubbish, is going to be transformed into a children's adventure playground.

The new minister, the Reverend Cedric Sheldrake, gave his first sermon on Sunday evening. The choir, led by Mrs Alberta Myers, sang: 'Who Is This, So Weak?'

You will be delighted to know that the former vicar, Reverend Basil Stitt, is recovering from his recent operation and is said to be fooling as well as he did before.

From a church festival programme:

Art Thou Troubled with the Boys Brigade Band (Handel)
I am going to my Bed (Unaccompanied)

From a Braintree newspaper:

The Archbishop yesterday condemned people that claimed members of the clergy do nothing more than gossip around a tea table. 'We have very real work to do,' he claimed. Afternoon tea was served as usual.

From a church notice:

ANYONE HAVING RELATIVES BURIED IN THE CHURCHYARD IS ASKED TO BE SO GOOD AS TO KEEP THEM IN ORDER.

From a Scottish newspaper:

The Reverend Angus McCann delivered the sermon, whilst a solo was sung by Miss Moira Macquiggan.

From a parish newsletter in Bromsgrove:

A special service of thanksgiving for the success of the recent campaign for distressed daughters of the clergy will be held in St Michael's followed by a beating in the Church Hall.

A clergyman was telling his congregation about the evil effects of drink and said: 'I hope that in time all liquor will be poured into the river. Now let us sing hymn number 162.' Unfortunately the title of hymn 162 was 'Let Us Gather at the River'.

Sign outside a church in Wandsworth:

EARTH'S FINAL WAR. WHERE WILL IT BE FOUGHT AND WHEN? At St John's Methodist Church, 8.00 p.m. on Tuesday.

EVENTS

2.30	Hymns of Praise. Films.
3.00	'HUNGRY MEN'
3.45	Question Time
4.00	Tea and Cakes
6.00	'I WAS SICK'
6.45	'WHAT DO WE DO?' – Open Forum
8.00	Prayers and Benediction

Correction:

The Vicar's talk to the women's meeting was not 'Smocking and rugs' as was reported, but 'Smoking and drugs'. We apologise for any embarrassment that may have resulted, especially to the ladies of the sewing circle who made the unnecessary journey.

From the Ely Standard Church News:

The concert in the Memorial Hall was a tremendous success and special thanks must go to Miss Colverson who played the piano for every item, which as usual fell upon her.

Sign seen hanging on a church door in Staffordshire:

THIS IS THE GATE OF HEAVEN ENTER YE ALL BY THIS DOOR.

(This door is kept locked because of the draught, please come round the back.)

Over thirty sacks of old clothing were sent to Miss Jonson in January, and we have just heard that she is using our gift in roofing the Church Mission House.

Correction to a Biblical manuscript:

Note that in John 15:13, 'wife' should read 'life'. Thus correcting: 'Greater love hath no man than this, that he lay down his wife for his friends.'

From a church magazine in Hull:

We are sorry to announce that Mr Albert Brown has been quite unwell, owing to his recent death, and is taking a short holiday to convalesce.

Notice outside a chapel:

The preacher next week will be the Reverend Humphrey Thomkins, after which the chapel will be closed for three weeks for repairs.

The service, taken by Reverend John Hamill, was at 11.00 a.m., his theme being EVIL MEMBER IN THE CHURCH. The choir sang the anthem: 'Who Can It Be?'

9 Inkling: a baby pen

If you deliberately want to make a mistake, then the Crazy Misstakes Dictionary is definitely for you. It is an international clanger dictionary, with daft definitions in so many languages you can't help but go RONG!

A

ab imo	*it belongs to him*
abito	*a piece of*
abyss	*an abbot's wife*
achtung	*my mouth hurts*
acme	*spots*
agape	*a big hole*
ahorros	*a four-legged animal used for racing*
amazon	*quite surprising*
antelope	*insect that runs off to get married*
anti-freeze	*a relative without her winter woollies*
apéritif	*set of dentures*
apocalypse	*a pocket-size lipstick*
asbestos	*as good as anyone else*

B

bacteria	*behind a café*
badminton	*reason the lamb tastes terrible*
balsam	*cry a lot*
Beau geste	*a very big joke*
bien	*French vegetable*
bizarre	*jumble sale*
blubber	*to whale*
boycott	*crib for baby boys*
brouhaha	*joy of French cooking*

C

caffe nero	*coffee with burning brandy on top*
carte blanche	*a white wheelbarrow*
catastrophe	*what a cat wins at a catshow*
chagrin	*cleaning lady's smile*
cistern	*container for toilet water*
clangour	*something you drop*
climate	*what you do with a ladder*
cloister	*extremely near to*
compos mentis	*a rotting brain*
congé	*a dance*
corpus	*dead body*
cul-de-sac	*out of the bag*

D

damnosa	*very inquisitive*
déjà vu	*nice to see you*
déjeuner	*travel*
désolé	*the bottom of a shoe*
dogwood	*forest for canines*
doldrums	*toy percussion instrument*
ductile	*what mallards have on the wall*

E

earwig	*muff for the ears*
e.g.	*what a hen lays*
en ami	*hostile person*
enosis	*he is very clever*
entourloupette	*the insane are on holiday*
eureka!	*you don't smell too pleasant*
extrados	*more please*
eyebrow	*very intellectual*

F

faggot	*a female maggot*
faux pas	*hostile father*
fête	*garden party that is worse than death*
fiasco	*Italian white wine*
fiddlesticks	*what you play a violin with*

flèche	skin
fruits de mer	seaweed
frustrate	the best you can get, very good indeed
fugue	very thick fog

G

galimafrée	Madam, I am not married
gallop	a pole
gangrene	not very experienced mob
germicide	viruses that kill themselves
granary	where your mother's mother lives
grande dame	very fat lady
guest	think about it
guise	slang term meaning 'men'

H

hasta la vista	you've got a nice view
hatless	the man that carried the world on his back
hermit	a woman's hand
hollywood	a prickly tree
hors concours	horse chestnut
hors de combat	fighting horses
hostel	what the enemy are
humbug	insect that can't sing
hymn	the opposite to her

I

idolise	tired eyes
igloo	eskimo toilet
impale	put in a bucket
infra dig	working on the garden
in loco parentis	on your parent's train
intense	what boy scouts sleep in
intermezzo	in a muddle
in toto	wearing a ballet skirt

J

jeu de mots	*I've got the moth*
jonquil	*murderer called John*
jugulate	*slow fetching the milk*
juno	*have you any idea*

K

kago	*the vehicle works*
kalmuck	*bovine dung*
karate	*a vegetable*
karma	*mother's transport*
kebbie	*taxi driver*
ketchup	*get level with the others*
kidnap	*the baby is asleep*
kukri	*preparing food*

L

lapsus memoriae	*poor memory*
largo	*Italian beer*
lattice	*green vegetable eaten by rabbits*
lemma	*fruit drink*
l'état c'est moi	*I am in a state*
living-room	*where you wouldn't be seen dead in*
logarithm	*dance for trees*

M

macaroni	*inventor of the radio*
magnum cum laude	*you'll have to turn the volume up*
magpie	*dessert made up of old papers*
maladie	*madam*
mal vu	*bad eyesight*
margin	*mother's favourite drink*
mauvais goût	*a bad leg*
mince	*sweets with holes in the middle*
mistral	*a singer who blacks his face*

N

nightingale	*stormy evening*
noblesse oblige	*nobody will help*
nom de plume	*called a feather*
notary	*paper money*
nun	*there isn't any*
nurture	*studying the countryside*

O

obiit	*get out*
oboe	*a tramp*
odium	*drug*
operetta	*girl who works for British Telecom*
O si sic omnes	*sea sickness*
overture	*someone who eats too much*

P

palaver	*a kind of cardigan or jumper*
palomine	*a friend of mine*
par excellence	*very good father*
pas de deux	*father of twins*
pharmacy	*growing crops*
piano	*shipping line*
pizzicato	*a baby pizza*
polonaise	*salad cream*
prawn	*smallest chess piece*
presto	*tight shoe*

Q

quaker	someone who shakes
quicksand	a fast hourglass
quod erat demonstrandum	demonstration by pest control officer

R

razor	wake her up
rechauffé	change around
rentier	give money to the landlord
rickets	what you knock down in cricket
roam	capital of Italy
romantic	insect from Italy
rugged	when you are sitting on the carpet
Russia	make you hurry
rut	decay
ruthless	we are without Ruth

S

shampoo	imitation poo
shamrock	fake stone
son et lumière	your son is alight
spider	she was seen

T

table d'hôte	hot plate
tertium quid	thirty pounds
touché	slightly mad
tour de force	troop inspection
transparent	mummy is in a trance
typhoon	millionaire

U

ultramarine	the best sailor
unison	the only boy
urchin	what is under 'er mouth
urdu	to have your hair done

V

vi et armis   *Vi has joined the territorials*
vixen   *the vicar's son*
viz   *face*

W

wedlock   *complete standstill*
winsome   *luck in a competition*

X

xerophyte   *is there a battle?*

Y

yarmulke   *here is your milk*
yashmak   *raincoat*

Z

zweifellos   *two men*

10 'Wanted: red-faced ladies' wrist-watch'

It pays to advertise, they say. But with advertisements becoming more and more expensive the cutting down of words in your advert can become more hysterical than economical (Three bed house, kitch, 2 beds near railway statn.), but if you don't make the mistake yourself then you'll find newspapers only too happy to make them for you.

'FOR SALE: Bicycle by lady with collapsible frame.'

New Zealand paper

'If you shoot yourself and have not tried Blank's ammunition, you have missed one of life's pleasures.'

Peterborough Weekly

'FOR SALE: To a good owner, fully grown and domesticated leopard. Able to roam free and untied. Will eat flesh from the hand. . . . Offers please.'

Calcutta newspaper

'HOUSEHOLD AND MISCELLANEOUS FOR SALE: High chair (converts to electric toaster) £10.50.'

Surrey Herald

'FOUR SINGLE POUND NOTES lost in area market on Tuesday night. Of sentimental value.'

Glasgow newspaper

'LADIES required for making of nurses' uniforms. A knowledge of upholstery would be an advantage.'
Evening Standard

'CHICKEN PORTIONS cooked in wine. All you need to eat the eat the eat the eat the all you need to do is eat the chicken whilst still in the bag. Ready in ten minutes.'
Pittsburgh Press

'FOR SALE: Sheraton table, property of titled lady, with exquisitely carved legs.'
New Homemaker

'OPAL-diamond ring, set in Hoovermatic de luxe twin tub £750 or nearest offer.'
Croydon Advertiser

'WANTED to trade one saxophone for cow in red leather case.'
Pueblo Chieftain

'FOR SALE: Four golden labrador puppies – good pedigree – £50 each to good home. Black Pedigree pram in good condition. Write Box 6784.'
Crawley & District Observer

'WANTED: first-class man fir rubbing-up and making good concrete faces.'
Norfolk paper

'WEST BRADFORD – freehold detached house – fitted kitchen (cooker, stainless steel sink unit, plumber in Hoover washing machine).'
Yorkshire evening paper

'LADY with deaf aid wishes to meet gentleman with contact lenses.'
Kern Valley Sun

'Grandad, 2 litre GL, 1979, 40,000 miles, good condition, fully taxed, one year's MOT. Offers please.'

Motor Car

'Fifteen foot travel trailer. Boat rack built on top, complete with wench.'

Practical Boat Owner

'FOUND small white Jack Russell terrier. Apply with name on collar to box 5694302.'

California paper

'TWO WHIPPET PUPS FOR SALE, 9 ft × 9 ft 6 in, all fittings on skids.'

Gloucester Citizen

'COOK WANTED: full board, two in family; only one who can be well recommended.'

Sutton Times

'HAMMERS for sale – bulk purchase, would suit any handyman with claw head.'

Dublin Evening Herald

'LADY with one child 3½ years old seeks employment as a housekeeper. God cook.'

The Lady

'BACHELOR (32), non-driver, would like to accompany someone similar on a car tour of Scottish highlands.'

Yorkshire evening paper

'MISS BRIMSTONE wishes it to be known that she has no male goat this season, and refers all clients to Mr Dobson.'

Suffolk paper

'DELIGHTFUL country cottage, 2 bedrooms, large lounge, diner kitchen, bathroom, coloured suite, toilet 5 miles from Chichester.'

Worthing Herald

'GOD is always at hand to help in times of trouble. Write Box No. 19986.'

Bedford paper

'RELIABLE and experienced baby-sister available. Ring any evening.'

Hampshire paper

'FOR SALE: mahogany Chip and Dale dining-room table, in excellent condition, reasonable.'

Antiques Weekly

'BEXHILL-ON-SEA. Semi detached house with sea through lounge.'

Sussex local paper

'Young lady required to work in office. Experience essential but not necessary.'

Kensington Post

'FOR SALE: Three-piece suite. Settee turns into bed covered in thick yellow mustard.'

Yellow Advertiser

'LIVESTOCK FOR SALE – two horses in perfect condition, hard body, fold away base. What am I offered?'

Yorkshire Post

'FOR SALE: beautiful silk wedding dress. Extra large size. Only worn twice.'

Kansas City News

'After the robbery the thieves must have realised that they had some very valuable and unique goods, most of them priceless antiques. The problem that faced them was how could they sell them?

> WHY NOT SELL IT THROUGH A SMALL
> ADVERTISEMENT IN THE HERALD?'

Australian paper

'SECRETARY requires work at home. Anything awful will be considered.'

Torquay Times

'FOR SALE: 1928 ROLLS-ROYCE HEARSE – original body.'

The Times

'PLEASE NOTE – you can order rings by post. State size or enclose string tied around your finger.'

Gloucester Citizen

'FOR SALE – DELICATE PORCELAIN STATUETTE. Victorian, belongs to elderly lady only slightly cracked.'

Essex Chronicle

'PRIVATE HOTEL, excellently situated near Bournemouth sea front. Practically on the level.'

Dorset paper

'HOUSE FOR SALE, complete with carpets, curtains, two double beds, washing machine, television, lion, etc.'

Plymouth paper

'OUR LADDERS will last over twenty years or more if you do not wear the rungs out with use.'

Liverpool Evening Express

'ACCOMMODATION includes large split-level lounge, with large bay window overlooking separate WC.'
Matlock Mercury

'FOR SALE three bar electric fire, with two bars working. Otherwise perfect.'
Tonbridge paper

'WANTED – to trade violin for shotgun.'
Portsmouth Evening News

'BRIDLINGTON. Comfortable apartments. Five minutes from the sea. Germs moderate.'
Yorkshire Evening Post

'WANTED – wet fish or experienced man or woman to run business.'
Norfolk paper

'NEW, a must for all students A GUIDE TO PUNCTUATION, and absolutely free! Simply send a large stamped-addressed envelope, marked PUNCIATION in the top left-hand corner.'
Acton Gazette

'AMAZING OFFER! Fish and chip fryer, made from chip-resistant enamel.'
Dalton's Weekly

'STRADIVARIUS violin for sale. Cheap. Almost new.'
Evening Standard

'WANTED – a reliable woman to cook, wash, iron and milk two cows.'
Farmers' Weekly

'One collapsible baby. Good condition. £15.'
Sheffield Telegraph

'LOST – an antique brooch depicting Venus in
Shepherd's Bush on Saturday night.'

Evening Standard

'IMPORTANT – if you purchased the do-it-yourself-
course *How to Fly a Plane in Ten Easy Lessons* you will
notice that the final section *How to land the Plane* has
been omitted owing to a printer's error. We apologise for
any inconvenience this may have caused you and if you
send us a stamped-addressed envelope we will send the
missing part to you as soon as we can.'

Detroit News

'GENTLEMEN with elasticated waists. Variety of colours.
All sizes.'

Daily Express

'Unusual opportunity for car salesman with initiative and
drive. Must have had at least two years' experience within
the last six months or do not apply.'

Manchester Evening News

'TO LET – young man two storeys, beautiful views,
balcony, full central heating.'

Paris newspaper

'LOST – almost white cat.'

Warwickshire paper

'C—'s CHEMIST will now be open from 1.30 to 5.30 p.m.
every afternoon, Monday to Friday for decapitated
student nurses.'

Nursing College Journal

'WANTED – first class male waitress.'

Montreal Star

'NEWSAGENT'S SHOP AND FLAT for sale. Occupier under notice to expire at the end of January.'
Surrey Comet

'TO LET – fully furnished apartment. Semi-private bathroom. Telephone evenings only.'
Hartsville Messenger

'ELECTRIC BLANKET for sale. Owner going abroad so no longer useful, pale green in colour.'
Bristol Evening Post

'PRECAST CONCRETE FOREMAN REQUIRED.'
Berkshire paper

'HORSE for sale complete with bridal, 6-volt battery, connecting rods, etc.'
New Zealand paper

'UNEMPLOYED MAN seeks work. Completely honest and trustworthy, will take anything.'
Farmers' Weekly

'Bonzoro Bay – luxury home, 3 bedrooms, septic tank not yet complete, owner still living in it.'
New Zealand paper

'SHEER silk stockings – designed for evening wear, but so serviceable that lots of women wear nothing else.'
Daily Mirror

'Owing to the fire at the Manor Lodge Hotel, guests are temporarily invited to stay at the Saxon Inn hotel where their welcome will be even warmer than before.'
Sussex local paper

'PIANIST wanted – both upright and grand.'
Canadian paper

'LADY, having spent Christmas with her family, can strongly recommend comfortable, quiet hotel.'

Pocklington Times

'FOR SALE – doctor's dinghy and accessories. Doctor no further use.'

Medical Times

'WAITRESS required for tea shop. Knowledge of first aid essential.'

Essex Weekly News

'Alsatian dog for sale. What am I offered for this beautiful young dog? Fully house-trained, gentle, will eat anything and is especially fond of children.'

Oxford Mail

'GIRL WANTED for petrol pump attendant.'

Kent paper

'Woman required for looking over fixed bats and cranks in warehouse.'

Lancashire evening paper

'AUSTRIAN/GERMAN/SWISS chefs required for new French restaurant.'

Evening Standard

93

'Small flatlet available mid-July, would suit two business ladies, use of communal kitchen or two gentlemen.'
Cumberland Herald

'FOR SALE lovely rosewood dining table. Owner going abroad with beautifully twisted legs.'
Manx Life

'WANTED – gas cooker suitable for bachelor with white enamelled sides.'
Evening News

'10 MILES FROM LONDON lovely little gentleman's weekend cottage.'
London paper

'TO LET, fully furnished flat. £200 per calendar month, electricity and rats included.'
Coventry Evening Telegraph

'KING OF MANX FAIRIES – £1.50 each – only this replica is the genuine and original model.'
Manx Life

'Young woman wants washing and cleaning three mornings a week.'
Lancashire Evening Telegraph

'Men's clothes brush, complete with leather zip case, and matching bomb set.'
Daily Express

'Widows made to order. Send us your specifications.'
Ely Standard

'BABY GRAND PIANO – would suit beginner with chipped legs.'
The Stage

'WANTED girls experienced for sticking on toothpicks.'
Oldham Evening Chronicle

'GENTS BICYCLE for sale, also two ladies in perfect working order.'
Cambridge Evening News

'Lady required to work six hours a week cleaning small officers in Station Road, Witney.'
Witney and West Oxfordshire Gazette

'You too can have confidence and comfort with your dentures if you sprinkle on Dr Thomkins' Powder every day. You can eat, laugh, talk, and enjoy your meals all day long. Forget your false teeth and start using Dr Thomkins' TODAY.'
Avon Advertiser

'Cordon bleu cook required for Government department dining-room. Good salary, excellent working conditions, plus luncheon vouchers.'
The Guardian

'THIS IS A GENUINE OFFER – No connection with any similar firm who are selling rubbish.'
From a circular

'FOR SALE: Quonset House in Douglas. Terms cash. All reasonable offers rejected.'
American Daily

'Surgical instruments: complete assortment of deceased surgeons.'
British Medical Journal

'DEEP FREEZE – best Scotch beef from Wales.'
Edinburgh Evening News

'I bought a few of your indigestion tablets last week and now I feel like a new man (original may be seen on request).'

Greenock Telegraph

'1982 Cortina, red with black roof, red interior, taxed with MOT, £1500, will consider smaller older car in part exchange for the wife.'

Braintree Advertiser

'Silk? Tweed? Hopsack? Worsted? No matter what your top coat is made of, this miracle spray will make it really repellent.'

Birmingham Evening Mail

'Baby's pushchair complete with baby, £15 only.'

Berkshire paper

'FOR SALE: Direct from the manufacturer, human hair wigs. Cut out the middle man – 100% cheaper.'

Sunday Express

'VINTAGE WINES for sale, property of elderly lady removed from cellar.'

London paper

'FOR SALE a cross cut saw by man with newly sharpened teeth.'

Farmers' Weekly

'Wanted – a house with garage or space for schoolmaster.'

Manchester Evening News

'FOR SALE: Granite-faced gentleman's residence in Brighton.'

Sussex paper

'PIANO for sale, quite cheap. The owner is getting grand.'

Music and Musicians

'WANTED: single room with bath for music lessons.'
Ayrshire Post

'NEW INSURANCE SCHEME: £3000 at death if within five years, with the option of continuing longer.'
Yorkshire paper

'The bank wish to announce that for improved customer service they will now be closed all day on Thursday.'
New York Times

'INVISIBLE MENDING. All customers are delighted with the results. A recent customer claimed that as a result of our work her garment did not look like a darned coat at all.'
Manchester Mercury

'NEEDED URGENTLY, new pair of football boots, for golden labrador puppy.'
California paper

'Save time and cut fingers with our new parsley mincer.'
Northern Daily Mail

'FOREMAN REQUIRED to take charge of ladies sandpapering turned legs.'
Crewe Weekly

'LETTUCE PLANTS, 50p per dozen, fitted with electric plug.'
Gardener's World

'LANDLORD has several flats let to tenants he wishes to dispose of.'
Liverpool Echo

11 'Ears pierced while you wait'

Some signs of the times can be very funny indeed. Here are some favourites that can be seen around the country.

Sign in Cornwall:
NO PERSON SHALL WALK, RUN, STAND, SIT OR LIE ON THE GRASS IN THIS PLEASURE GROUND.

Sign outside a hotel:
WAITRESSES REQUIRED FOR BREAKFAST – APPLY INSIDE.

Seen in a London department store:
BARGAIN BASEMENT UPSTAIRS.

Notice outside a church hall:
2.30 p.m. WOMEN ARE REVOLTING
Special film and talk.
All invited.

Sign on an electricity pylon:
DANGER!
TO TOUCH THESE WIRES WILL RESULT IN INSTANT DEATH. ANYONE FOUND DOING SO WILL BE SEVERELY PROSECUTED.

Notice on a Hong Kong beach:
NO GAMES
KEEP BEACH CLEAR FOR LITTERS

Sign in aircraft assembly factory:
HOLES PAINTED WHITE ARE NOT TO BE DRILLED.

A Women's Institute displayed the following in their window:
THE EVENING OF CLAIRVOYANCE ON THURSDAY 26 NOVEMBER, AT 7.30 p.m. HAS BEEN CANCELLED DUE TO UNFORESEEN CIRCUMSTANCES.

Notice in a hotel bedroom:
IF YOU REQUIRE A BATH RING FOR THE CHAMBERMAID.

Seen on the edge of a lake in Cumbria:
ANY PERSON PASSING BEYOND THIS POINT WILL BE DROWNED.
By order of the magistrates.

From a confectioner's window in Yorkshire:
IF IT'S SWEETS YOU WANT THEN TRY US. THE BEST IS NEVER TOO GOOD FOR YOU.

Sign in an American veterinary surgery:
CAPITAL PET ANIMAL HOSPITAL
Dogs called for, fleas removed and returned to you the same day. Three dollars.

Seen in a children's playground:
COMPETITION – WIN A DAY AT LONDON ZOO WITH LUNCH THROWN IN!

Notice outside a dance hall:

SATURDAY NIGHT DISCO
Very Exclusive
Everybody is welcome

Sign on a Torquay hotel:

CAUTION!
THIS HOTEL IS FULLY LICENSED AND SITUATED
ON THE EAST CLIFF.

From an electrical shop:
WHY BREAK YOUR CHINA WASHING UP?
Do it automatically in a dishwasher!

Outside a disco:
COME IN YOUR THOUSANDS! Hall holds 500.

Notice in a Sunderland chemists:
WE DISPENSE WITH ACCURACY.

A laundry offers:
EVERY THURSDAY WE OFFER ALL OLD AGE
PENSIONERS A FREE SOAP, BLEACH AND DRY,
PLUS HOT STEAM PRESS TO MAKE ANYTHING YOU
HAVE LOOK LIKE NEW.

SAME DAY CLEANERS! 48-HOUR SERVICE.
We do not tear your clothes with machinery. We do it
carefully by hand.

LOST – White beagle dog answers to the name of
'SCHNOOK'. Is old blind and deaf. REWARD for return.

URGENTLY NEEDED – WOMAN TO SEW BUTTONS
ON THE FIFTH FLOOR.

ALMA'S LAUNDRY – LEAVE ALL YOUR CLOTHES
HERE, LADIES, AND SPEND THE AFTERNOON
SHOPPING.

STAFF SHOULD EMPTY THE TEAPOT AND THEN
STAND UPSIDE DOWN ON THE DRAINING BOARD
PLEASE.

From a Suffolk farm:
ANY DOGS FOUND WORRYING WILL BE SHOT.

Sign in washing-machine shop in Walsall:
DON'T KILL YOUR WIFE. LET OUR WASHING
MACHINES DO ALL THE DIRTY WORK!

WE INFORM ALL HAULIERS AND CITIZENS WHO
HAVE CATTLE THAT THEIR PRESENCE IN A
DRUNKEN CONDITION IN STATIONS AND TRAINS IS
STRICTLY FORBIDDEN AND THEY WILL BE
BANNED.

HAIRCUTTING WHILE YOU WAIT.

CUSTOMERS GIVING ORDERS WILL BE PROMPTLY
EXECUTED.

LARGE ELEPHANT WAGON FOR SALE – HOLDS
TWO ELEPHANTS OR WOULD SUIT SHOWMAN.

MODEL REQUIRED – WILLING TO POSE FOR NUDE ARTIST.

TO THE FAIRY GLEN
5 minutes walk
BEWARE OF HEAVY LORRIES

THE SALISBURY HOUSE HOTEL
Every Thurs and Sat
Come dancing to the Salisbury Band (all aged).

If you are willing to pay just a little more and are looking for a really fascinating out-of-the-ordinary pet, may we suggest you try the second floor and ask to see Miss Osborne.

FOAM CUSHIONS AT ROCK BOTTOM PRICES.

PIERCED EARS £1.50 A PAIR.

Sign outside hospital ward:
VISITORS
HUSBANDS ONLY. ONE PER PATIENT.

ONCE YOU HAVE DEALT WITH US YOU WILL SOON RECOMMEND OTHERS.

MOUSE TO LET

THE CHANCELLOR OF THE EXCHEQUER WILL SPEAK AT THE CONSERVATIVE CLUB GARDEN PARTY ON SATURDAY.
Beware of pickpockets.

Spotted recently near Colchester:
GO SLOW – CONCEALED ROAD ENTRANCE.
NO OVERTAKING FOR NEXT 200 YRS

Sign outside pub in America:
GENUINE ENGLISH PUB, SERVING SCONES.

NOTICE
No cars or cycles
on this footpath
is prohibited.

WE EXCHANGE EVERYTHING – COOKERS,
WASHING MACHINES, FRIDGES,
Etc. Etc. Etc.
BRING YOUR WIFE AND GET THE
DEAL OF YOUR LIFE.

Our charges are equal to quality and can safely be said
what you get here will be the lowest in the area.

*In a large park in Ohio there is a small bandstand, around
which are many seats. A sign states:*
The seats in this vicinity are for the use of ladies.
Gentlemen should sit on them only after the former are
seated.

PIANO LESSONS – SPECIAL PAINS ARE GIVEN TO
BEGINNERS.

Sign in dry cleaners:
CUSTOMERS LEAVING GARMENTS LONGER THAN
THIRTY DAYS WILL NOW BE DISPOSED OF.

WANTED – MAN TO WASH DISHES AND TWO
WAITRESSES.

MONDAY 6.30 p.m. *What is Hell?* Tip-up seats.
Everybody is welcome.

CUSTOMERS WHO CONSIDER OUR WAITERS ARE
RUDE SHOULD SEE THE MANAGERESS.

BOAT FOR SALE: ONLY ONE OWNER. YELLOW IN COLOUR.

TOILETS OUT OF ORDER
Please use platforms 7 and 11

MORRIS'S RESTAURANT WHERE GOOD FOOD IS AN UNEXPECTED PLEASURE.

WHY GO ANYWHERE ELSE AND BE CHEATED WHEN YOU CAN COME HERE?

Sign seen in a Hawaiian dress-shop window:
YOU WILL NEVER FIND BETTER OR MORE EXCITING BIKINIS THAN OURS – THEY ARE SIMPLY THE TOPS!

From a school in Derbyshire:
WILL THE INDIVIDUAL WHO BORROWED A LADDER FROM THE CARETAKER LAST MONTH KINDLY RETURN SAME IMMEDIATELY OTHERWISE FURTHER STEPS WILL BE TAKEN.

THE ROYAL BULLET COMPANY PRESENT *SWAN LAKE*

ONE WEEK SALE OF SHEETS
These bargains are rapidly shrinking.

EASTER FLOWER SERVICE
Parents and adult fiends are invited.

In a theatre the following sign was situated a little too close to the lavatories for comfort:
PATRONS ARE REQUESTED TO REMAIN SEATED THROUGHOUT THE ENTIRE PERFORMANCE.

PARTIES UP TO 1000 CAN AND HAVE BEEN DONE.

On the Thames near Henley:
DANGER – When red flags are flying flooding of the river is imminent and members of the public must not leave the river banks.

Notice seen in the vicinity of Victoria Station:
CLOSED FOR OFFICIAL OPENING

WET CLEANER REQUIRED FOR DRY CLEANERS

As from next Thursday, the catering assistants will serve customers to all potatoes.

Notice on Southend pier:
DON'T THROW
PEOPLE BELOW

TRY OUR SUPERIOR BUTTER – NOBODY CAN TOUCH IT.

BUY OUR DELICIOUS CREAM – IT CAN'T BE BEATEN.

BABY SHOW – ENTRIES TO BE HANDED IN AT THE GATE.

Sign in clothing shop:
GIRLS READY TO WEAR CLOTHES

OUR MOTTO IS TO GIVE OUR CUSTOMERS THE VERY LOWEST PRICES AND WORKMANSHIP.

OSCAR'S FUNERAL PARLOUR – the service with a smile.

LOST at the meat market – bloodhound.

12 The Crazy Misstakes Quiz

So far we have looked at the mistakes of other people, but now it is time to look at your mistakes! Here is a quick quiz to test your capacity for making mistakes and spotting errors. If you can answer all the questions without one single blunder, you could be the most perfickt person in the world!

1 If on the last day of February 1980 – and remember it was a leap year – you had gone to bed at seven o'clock, having set the alarm to wake you up at 8.15 a.m., how much sleep would you have got?

2 Copy down the following sentence *A bird in the the hand is worth two in the bush.*

3 An archaeologist recently claimed that he had found a coin dated 46 BC. Do you think he did?

4 If red houses are made out of red bricks and yellow houses are made out of yellow bricks, what are green houses made out of?

5 Which is correct? Nine and five *are* thirteen OR nine and five *is* thirteen?

6 What is it that occurs four time in every week, twice in every month, but only once in a year?

7 Their are five mistaikes in this sentence. Can you spot them?

8 Here are twenty facts. Which are false?

(a) The African elephant always sleeps standing up, which means that it is on its feet for over fifty years.

(b) In Iceland families do not have surnames.

(c) Seaweed is used in the manufacture of toothpaste and icecream.

(d) A kangaroo cannot jump with its tail off the ground.

(e) Our Queen Elizabeth II is the first monarch to have been born in a private house.

(f) 'Cha' is the Chinese word for tea.

(g) Peanuts are used in the manufacture of dynamite.

(h) Gorillas are vegetarians.

(i) There are 2000 species of parsley.

(j) Ostriches can swim.

(k) It is impossible to make colourless wine.

(l) In China a soup is made from birds' nests.

(m) Cats spend two-thirds of their lives asleep.

(n) Otters can jump into water without making a splash.

(o) Elephants cannot jump.

(p) The largest eggs are laid by sharks.

(q) In America there are 8 different cities called Rome.

(r) Shakespeare's daughter could not read or write.

(s) Mushrooms can grow through concrete.

(t) The human body has 206 bones.

9 Which is the odd one out in the following groups?

(a) Lynx, puma, leopard, coyote, ocelot.

(b) Matthew, John, Mark, Luke, Peter.

(c) John, Paul, Ginger, Ringo, George.

(d) Gaelic, Urdu, Swahili, Latin, Origami.

(e) Fagin, Falstaff, Steerforth, Squeers, Micawber.

(f) Hoover, Chrysler, Carter, Reagan, Ford.

(g) Pearl, topaz, amethyst, diamond, emerald.

(h) Taurus, Orion, Libra, Scorpio, Sagittarius.

10 Is it possible to add five lines to the six lines shown here and make nine?

11 A little girl was given one 50p piece to buy some sweets by her mother, and another 50p piece to buy some fruit. When she got to the gate, however, she started to cry. Why? She still had both 50p pieces.

12 Answer the following questions:
   (a) Why should you always remain calm when you meet cannibals?
   (b) When does a timid girl turn to stone?
   (c) What is the best way to keep loafers from standing on the street corner?
   (d) If you woke up in the night feeling sad, what would you do?
   (e) Three copycats were sitting on a cliff and one jumped off. How many were left?
   (f) Why did the moron throw all his nails away?
   (g) Why must a dishonest man stay indoors?
   (h) Why is an honest friend like crystallised fruit?
   (i) What should we give to people who are too breezy?
   (j) What kind of vice is it that people dislike if they are bad?

NOW see how many mistakes you made. . . .

13 'Put minced steam in bowl ...'

There is absolutely no area in which man cannot make a mistake, whether it is writing a letter or simply putting out a note for the milkman. Here are some miscellaneous mistakes from a variety of sauces ... sorry, sources!

'After removing your lunch from the saucepan allow it to soak in very hot soapy water. . . .'

Instructions on a fruit jar:
TO OPEN JAR, PIERCE WITH A PIN TO RELEASE VACUUM – THEN PUSH OFF.

From 'Woman's Weekly' Film Offer pre-paid envelope:

No stamp needed but for fastest service we suggest a first class stamp.

Note to a schoolteacher:
Dear Sir,
Please ixcuse Arold from skool today. He kant cum cos he is acting as timekeeper for his dad and it is awl your folt. His

homework sed if a field is 1o miles round, how long will it take a man walking 3 miles an hour to walk round it 1o times. Arold aint a man so we sent his father. His father is walking round while Arold times im so please don't give im homework like that no more cos his dad as to go to work.

From yours,
Arold's Mum.

Label on bottle:

FLIES COMING INTO CONTACT WITH THIS PREPARATION DIE WITHOUT HOPE OF RECOVERY.

Some samples from the 'Readers' Queries' page of a magazine:

'How can you make household starch?'

'Quite simply by adding two tablespoons of cold water to three tablespoons of water. Mix into a paste. Add boiling water until starch appears.'

'What can I do with leftover fruit juice?'

'Mix it with a cupful of sugar, half a cup of cornflour, and two egg yolks. Delicious on kids' shoes.'

'How can you tell the age of a frog?'

'It is difficult to tell a frog's age, unless you happen to know when it was born.'

Letter to a customer:

Dear Sir,

We are sorry that we have not been able to supply you with the items you required, but due to increased demand our stocks are very low. Fortunately we are expecting further delays any time now.

Yours,

Another note to a schoolteacher:

Please do not force Ethel to have cabbage at dinner time.
She only comes home with it in her sock.

From a travel brochure:

From this valley you travel southwards, growing much
more beautiful as you go along.

From a book of etiquette:

It is considered very bad manners to tear off bits of beard
and dip them in your soup.

From a Women's magazine in America:

SUET PUDDING: Many people do not have great success
with suet puddings. They should be steamed.

Letter from a travel agent:

Dear Sir,
I am afraid the flight you wanted is fully booked, but if
someone falls out we will let you know.

From a Women's Institute newsletter:

A competition was held to find the most unusual object. The winner was Marjorie Reilly.

From an insurance policy:

This policy will help you recover from any kind of fatal accident.

Wedding invitation:

> Mr & Mrs Alfred Pearson
> request the honour of your presents
> at the marriage of their daughter
> George
> to
> Mr Neville Wilson.

From a novel:

He looked very broad across the shoulders, almost as if there was too much pudding in his jacket.

From a textbook:

At between 500°C and 550°C the substance becomes completely pliable and could be moulded in the hands like Plasticine.

From a brochure giving details of facilities:

It is to easy to slip on a polished floor and so a special floor has been laid with this end in view.

From a clothing catalogue:

If you want a garment that will wear well, choose one that is hard-wearing.

From a cookery book:

Put minced steam in bowl and make a hole in the centre to let the steam out.

Instructions on waste-disposal unit:

Tip your food off the plate down the drain and the machine will grind it up into easily digestible pieces.

From a first aid book:

The first thing to do when treating burns is to make sure the patient is removed from the fire.

From an Australian recipe book:

This delicious savoury sauce can be made up to half an hour before the meal, but should be served piping hot in a gravy boat so that your guests can pour it over themselves.

Household hint:

Ink can be more easily removed from white tablecloths before it is spilt than after.

From a women's magazine:

For a party such as this, to save washing-up, produce food that can easily be eaten using only a fork. You will find in the winter months that a clear soup goes down awfully well.

Reply to a customer's letter of complaint:

Dear Madam,
With reference to the raincoat you returned to us. The manufacturers have tested it and find it fully waterproof. Wear it on a dry day, take it off and turn it inside out and you will find that they are right.

To make a sponge cake:

Mix equal amounts of flour and sugar to a pinch of baking powder; break an egg into a cup and slide into the mixture.

Letter from welfare organisation for animals:

Dear Sir,

We are always happy to advise on getting rid of pests painlessly but in your case this really does not appear to be necessary. . . .

Instructions with a new car:

WHEEL CHANGING – the square wheel can be found at the back of the boot of your car.

Cooking tip:

Wash onions carefully and boil for ten minutes. After this, swim out into a pan of cold water and with your fingers pull the skin off. This stops the smell and will therefore prevent you crying.

From a novel:

'I'm sorry I forget your name, Mr Papa . . . pap . . .' she stumbled over the words, as Richard reached out his hand and helped her to her feet. She had been sitting with her head in her hands and her eyes on the floor until he arrived.

How to cook fresh corn:

Spread ears with butter, or let each guest butter their own ears before they start.

A letter to the milkman:

Dear milkman,
My baby arrived yesterday.
Please leave another one.

High Tide tomorrow: 3.30 a.m.
Sunrise: 4.37 a.m.
Checked by the police who had to use force.

Correction:

We wish to put right the *Medical Journal*'s advertisement
in last week's paper. It should have read 'Talk on eye
screening' and not 'Talk on ice cream' as we stated. We
apologise for this oversight.

Another reply to a letter of complaint:

Dear Madam,
We are sorry that your gas boiler does not give you
sufficient hot water for a bath. I will go into this with you as
soon as I can.

> Yours faithfully,
> MANAGER

Shipping line leaflet:

By coming away with us for the winter you will find the
colder months less depressing for others as well as
yourself.

Instructions:

Pour a teaspoonful of liquid into the palm of each
hand. . . .'

14 'Einstein, you will never amount to much. . . .'

Finally, here are the biggest clangers of all time, proving that not only is the pen mightier than the sword, but the tongue can be mightier than the mouth, and nobody's mouth is so small that they can't put their foot right in it. These major calamities show that life may be cruel, but it's certainly comic.

If anyone in Britain will be remembered for achievements in the 1970s it is certain that Margaret Thatcher will be amongst them as the first woman Prime Minister. Not noted for being unsure of herself, Mrs Thatcher would most surely blush were she to be reminded of something she said in 1969:

'No woman in my time will be Prime Minister. Anyway, I wouldn't want to be Prime Minister. . . .'

William Langdon had been invited to a fancy dress party in Surrey, and decided to go as a chicken, but unfortunately got lost on the way. He came across an open air perform- ance of Winnie the Pooh *and, thinking that this was the party, he leapt amongst the actors and began clucking like a hen. He was arrested for disturbing the peace.*

Presidents of the United States are noted for making more slips than British Prime Ministers, and President Ronald Reagan is no exception. He is, nevertheless, on equal footing with Margaret Thatcher, for in 1973 he said:

'The thought of being President frightens me, I do not think I would want the job.'

In America a new cookery book appeared on the market containing a delicious recipe for Caramel Slices. It was an easy recipe to make, the main ingredient being a can of condensed milk, which the recipe book said should be placed in a saucepan and heated for four hours. The book omitted to say anything about putting water in the pan too – and without water it would explode.

Every copy of the book had to be recalled, making it one of the most expensive recipe books ever – for the publishers.

As long as man has been on the earth he has made mistakes, and any kind of modern invention has always been treated with more than a little suspicion. One Dr Dionysus Lardner, a professor of philosophy and astronomy at University College, London, claimed in the nineteenth century that rail travel would be impossible because passengers would be unable to breathe if they travelled at high speeds. Likewise he felt that no ship would ever be able to cross the Atlantic because the weight of coal it would need would cause it to sink. Were he still around he would be forced to eat his words.

For a recent exhibition by the Royal Society for the Prevention of Accidents, some special display shelves were put up. Shortly after the exhibition opened, the shelves collapsed, injuring one of the visitors.

Unemployed labourer Robin Gordon was discovered inside his local bank in the early hours of the morning. When asked by police what he was doing there, 'I came to pay my overdraft,' was his reply.

In 1932 a couple went shopping in London. It was close to Christmas and they visited all the West End stores. At the end of the day they returned home by taxi, loaded down with large parcels. When they got home they seemed to have one package too many, and on opening it, to their absolute astonishment, they found it to be a jewellery box filled with diamonds and rubies and countless other precious stones. They immediately took it to the nearest police station, and the jewels were later valued at over a quarter of a million pounds – several million pounds by today's standards.

Surprisingly enough, nobody claimed them. The police eventually managed to trace the owner, a Russian Grand Duchess. The stones had been part of the Russian crown jewels and nobody had even noticed that they were missing.

People are not the only ones to make mistakes, animals can too. A cat called Percy discovered a mouse drinking from his saucer of milk, and when he approached the mouse bit him on the nose. Percy fled away in terror and later had to be taken to the vet, who put a plaster right across the cat's nose. Not only was his nose hurt but his pride was too, and Percy now hides if he sees a mouse!

A nineteenth-century art critic called John Hunt made a slight error of judgement. Criticising the works of Rembrandt he said: 'Rembrandt is not to be compared in the painting of character with our extraordinarily gifted English artist, Mr Rippingille.' A century later, however, how many people can boast that they own a Rippingille? Not many, we're glad to say.

A well-known actress, who for obvious reasons wishes to remain anonymous, was once giving a cocktail party and had a little too much to drink. Halfway through the party she saw three guests coming towards her. She assumed they were leaving because they were carrying their coats, but actually they had just arrived. Staggering up to them she said: 'Oh, must you stay? Can't you go?'

After being arrested for a breach of the peace, it was discovered by the police that Michael Smith had given them a false name.

'I didn't think they would believe me if I told them my name was Smith,' he said. He had told them his name was Jones.

In 1925, when Calvin Coolidge had been elected President of the United States, he invited a few friends to dine with him at the White House. The guests felt very uneasy in such grand surroundings and in order to ensure that they did everything correctly they decided to copy everything that Coolidge did.

After the meal the President poured half his coffee into his saucer – so his guests did the same. He then poured cream into the coffee and added sugar. The guests did likewise. The President then knelt down and laid his saucer on the floor for the cat.

In 1978, Mr James Callaghan, then British Prime Minister, was invited to open the new premises of the Anglo-Austrian Society and to unveil a plaque to commemorate the occasion. The photographers gathered around with cameras poised, waiting for the moment when the plaque was to be unveiled. As Mr Callaghan pulled the string, the plaque fell off the wall.

119

Edward Hargreaves, in 1982, lost a finger whilst operating some machinery in the factory where he worked. Before the insurance company would pay him any money, they said that the machine must first be inspected. A few days later a man from the insurance company arrived and asked to test the machine. He too lost a finger. The insurance company paid Mr Hargreaves his money without further questioning.

Clyde Hunter and Marcia Brown had a memorable wedding day, thanks to an error of judgement on the part of the photographer. Deciding to take one final picture of the happy couple, the photographer asked them to step backwards a few paces. They did so, and shot over the edge of the balcony on which they were standing, into a lake some six metres below. They were still holding hands when they were rescued, and spent a six-month honeymoon in hospital – in separate wards.

The BBC in London has one of the greatest libraries of recorded sound effects in the world, and whatever the play or broadcast, an appropriate sound effect can be found, whether it is of a baby crying or a window breaking, the footsteps of an African elephant walking through a swamp or a rocket taking off to the moon. Nothing is beyond them. So, when the King of Norway was going to broadcast to the nation, finding an official fanfare seemed no problem, except for the small fact that the Sound Effects Department read the order as 'funfair' not 'fanfare'! Instead of being introduced by trumpets, the King was greeted with a loud cry of: 'Roll up! Roll up! All the fun of the fair . . .' and a barrel organ playing *Over the Waves*.

A British Ambassador had been invited to a very exclusive dinner party at the American Embassy, and to emphasise a point he was making during a discussion he began to wave his arms around frantically. Unfortunately his arm brushed against the head of the host's wife, sending her hair flying across the room and revealing that she was completely bald.

Everybody thinks of Florence Nightingale, the 'lady with the lamp', as being one of the greatest nurses of all time. Few people know that she was one of the greatest hypochondriacs of all time too! When she was 47 she thought she was dying. Feeling that her life hung by a single thread, she took to her bed and stayed there – for another 43 years, dying at the age of 90!

In 1882 the outlaw, Jesse James, was killed during a gunfight when he and his gang tried to rob a bank. The shooting began when the cashier refused to unlock the safe. Jesse James was killed in the shoot-out, and died not knowing that the safe had actually been open all the time.

In February 1981, dustman Brian Brooks opened his garage door expecting to see the £700 worth of property that he had stored there – two electric motors, a washing machine, a television set, a sun lounger, a work bench, car jacks, ramps and various tools. Instead he found it completely empty. Local council workmen had been along, cleared the garage and allocated it to someone else. A mistake was made over the garage numbering and the council had emptied the wrong garage! Unfortunately the council had since distributed the property all around the country.

Graham Swadling of Rye, Sussex, was delighted when he found a duck's egg one morning and took it home for his breakfast. Finding it to be very tasty indeed, he wrote a letter to his local newspaper telling them what a delicious breakfast duck's eggs made. The letter was published. Mr Swadling was later prosecuted under section 1c of the Protection of Birds Act 1954, which says that to eat the egg of a wild duck is an offence.

One of the most spectacular military clangers occurred in 1862 during the American Civil War when one General Ambrose Burnside ordered his troops to cross a river by means of a very narrow bridge. Because of the bridge's width, the soldiers could only move across very slowly and no more than two abreast, the result being that they became an easy target for the enemy and were all shot.

Had the General been more observant he would have noticed that the river was only a few inches deep and the troops could easily have walked through it unseen.

President Lincoln paid tribute to Burnside saying: 'Only he could wring spectacular defeat out of the jaws of victory.'

In 1969, scientist and electrician Reuben Tice set about inventing a machine that would iron the wrinkles out of prunes. One evening there was a very large explosion and Reuben was killed as bits of his machine were blasted all over the workshop. Beside his body lay half-a-pound of wrinkled prunes.

In 1919 during the Peace Conference at Versailles, David Lloyd George came up with the marvellous suggestion that the Italian Government could replace the commercial losses they had suffered during World War I by increasing their banana production. In theory the idea was a very good one apart from one minor snag . . . they don't grow bananas in Italy.

Mr Walter Brunsen made the mistake of trying to swindle the Gas Board by using the same coin in his meter over and over again for two years. When he was eventually found out he told the police: 'I did it on the spur of the moment.'

In one of his portraits of Charles I, Anthony Van Dyck painted the king with two gauntlets. Both of them were for the right hand.

A woman in Germany made the error of trying to steal a chicken out of her local supermarket without paying for it. It was a frozen chicken and she hid it under her hat. Within a few minutes she collapsed on the floor and was rushed to hospital with suspected brain damage.

After an all-night party, Miss Tina Houlst and Mr Barry Angus were driving home in his new sports car through the countryside. After a few miles, Mr Angus fell asleep at the wheel, the car went out of control, shot down a bank, rolled over and crashed into a tree. As they climbed from the wreckage unscathed, they looked at the crumpled car.

With relief, Miss Houlst exclaimed: 'Thank goodness we weren't hurt!'

Furious at the damage to his new car, Mr Angus slammed the door in disgust and chopped two of his fingers off.

A television camera crew from the BBC one day arrived at a remote farmhouse to film what was believed to be the oldest duck in the world. They spent a marvellous day filming the creature, and enjoyed their day on the farm. At the end of the day, with plenty of films made of the duck, they packed all their equipment in the van and set off down the lane towards the main road. Turning to wave farewell to the farmer and his wife the driver didn't look where he was going and ran over something. It was the duck.

They say that crime never pays, and certainly in two cases in America it didn't! In one instance a robber drew out a gun and said to the cashier: 'I am a bank robber – hand over the money.' At which point the man standing behind him in the queue drew out a gun, saying 'I am a policeman and you are being arrested for attempted robbery.' Another robber, in Pennsylvania, went into a bank armed with a toy gun, and pushed a note to the cashier. The note said: '1 lb sausages, 1 pint of milk, 1 tin of peas.' Realising his mistake, the would-be robber fled!

Many people feel that they should not draw attention to themselves in public. Mrs Vera Clyne is no exception. When her son Robert accidentally got his head stuck in a vase, as she took him on the bus to have it removed by the hospital, she placed his school cap on top of the vase hoping that nobody would notice his predicament. Unfortunately it didn't work!

In 1864, during the Battle of Spotsylvania in the American Civil War, one General Sedgwick peered over a parapet, and sneering at the enemy said: 'They couldn't hit an elephant at this dist. . . .'

They were his last words.

After the film *The Wizard of Oz* was first shown the critics claimed that the 'rainbow song should be cut' because it was too long. Over forty years later the film is still as popular as ever, and the most memorable song is, of course, 'Somewhere Over the Rainbow'. Well, first impressions aren't always right!

Mrs Ivy Beasley went to a portrait photographer because he claimed outside that it was 'While-You-Wait' photography. After her picture was taken, however, she was told to come back the next day to collect the picture. When Mrs Beasley questioned the 'While-You-Wait' claim she was told it meant the picture was taken while you waited, but it took a day to get it developed! Don't make the mistake of believing all you read. . . .

On 25 November 1952, Agatha Christie's thriller *The Mousetrap* opened in London. 'It might run a year . . .' said the playwright. Agatha Christie died in 1976. The play is still running!

In May 1982 a poisonous cobra bit 22-year-old Audrey Ruskin on the leg – the snake died.

A young actor once auditioned for a film called *The Front Page*, but was turned down for the part because the director said his ears were too big and that he looked like a taxi with the doors open. Later the actor was chosen to play a leading role in one of the greatest films ever made, *Gone With The Wind*. The actor's name was Clark Gable.

That famous knighted-goon, Sir Cumferance himself, Sir Harry Secombe was once invited to perform before the inmates of Pentonville Prison. The concert went very well until he sang his well-loved rendition of Bless This House, *which was slightly unfortunate as it contains the words: 'Bless these walls so firm and stout, keeping want and trouble out. . . .'*

Baby-sitter Bridget Buett made a bit of a bloomer when looking after newly-born identical twins one evening. They had been kept in separate cots so that they could be identified, and Bridget somehow managed to muddle the two up. The parents had to take the babies back to hospital for a check of their footprints so that they could tell which was which!

In 1937, a man called William Hitler said of his Uncle Adolf, 'My uncle is a peaceful man. He thinks war is not worth a candle.' A year later, Britain was at war with Germany because of Adolf Hitler.

In 1972, a Durham housewife decided to clean the floor of her budgie's cage, making the mistake of leaving the budgie in the cage while she did so, and the even bigger mistake of using a vacuum cleaner for the job. The last she saw of her pet was a few feathers floating through the air as the bird shot up her Hoover pipe.

In April 1975 two passengers of a light aircraft were killed as their plane crashed into a billboard. The unfortunate message on the board was 'Learn to Fly'.

Solutions to Quiz

1   Assuming you do not have a twenty-four hour alarm clock, you will get just 1¼ hours rest before the alarm goes off.

2   If you copied the proverb down correctly you should have made the mistake of including 'the' twice in succession.

3   In 46 BC they would have no idea that Christ was to be born and so it is impossible to find a coin with that date on it.

4   Green houses are made out of glass!

5   Neither is correct: nine and five equal fourteen!

6   The letter 'e'.

7   The mistakes are:
   (1) 'Their' instead of 'There'.
   (2) 'Mistaikes' instead of 'mistakes'.
   (3) 'Sentance' instead of 'sentence'.
   (4) The fact that there are four mistakes, not five!

8   None are false, they are all TRUE!

9   (a) Coyote. (b) Peter. (c) Ginger. (d) Origami.
   (e) Falstaff. (f) Chrysler. (g) Pearl. (h) Orion.

10   Yes!

11   Because she had forgotten which 50p was for the fruit and which for the sweets.

12   (a) So you don't get in a stew. (b) When she becomes a little bolder. (c) Give them a chair. (d) Look on the bed for a comforter. (e) None. (f) Because the heads were on the wrong end. (g) He can't go far while lying. (h) Because he's candid (candied). (i) The air. (j) Ad-vice.

More Beaver Books

We hope you have enjoyed this Beaver Book. Here are some of the other titles:

Crazy Graffiti A Beaver original. A hilarious book packed with examples of graffiti from the classroom, the playground, the shops, the cinema and so on, drawn on a number of different 'wall' backgrounds. Written by Janet Rogers, author of the Beaver *Crazy Joke* book series, and illustrated by David Mostyn

The Beaver Book of Crazy Hoaxes A Beaver original. You may have heard about the man who sold the Eiffel Tower, but what about the Cambridge students who fooled the Royal Navy, or the TV programme about the spaghetti harvest? These are just some of the incredible tricks hoaxers have played which are described in this book by Joseph Brundene, author of *The Beaver Book of Crazy Inventions*. Illustrated by Graham Thompson

The Beaver Book of Tongue Twisters A Beaver original. Can you say 'the Leith police dismisseth us' or 'Rory Rumpus rode a rawboned racer'? Here are tongue twisters of all kinds – old and new, long and short, difficult and easy – to keep you amused for hours. Written by Janet Rogers and illustrated by Graham Thompson

These and many other Beavers are available from your local bookshop or newsagent, or can be ordered direct from: Hamlyn Paperback Cash Sales, PO Box 11, Falmouth, Cornwall TR10 9EN. Send a cheque or postal order made payable to the Hamlyn Publishing Group, for the price of the book plus postage at the following rates:
UK: 45p for the first book, 20p for the second book, and 14p for each additional book ordered to a maximum charge of £1.63;
BFPO and Eire: 45p for the first book, 20p for the second book, plus 14p per copy for the next 7 books and thereafter 8p per book;
OVERSEAS: 75p for the first book and 21p for each extra book.

New Beavers are published every month and if you would like the *Beaver Bulletin*, a newsletter which tells you about new books and gives a complete list of titles and prices, send a large stamped addressed envelope to:

Beaver Bulletin
Arrow Books Limited
17-21 Conway Street
London W1P 6JD

9366606